THE WEAPON
CHAINING THE GATES OF HELL WITH THE HOLY ROSARY

BY

MICHAEL VORIS, S.T.B.

ST. MICHAEL'S MEDIA PUBLISHING

For permission requests, write to:

St. Michael's Media Publishing
2840 Hilton Road
Ferndale, MI 48220

www.ChurchMilitant.com

Printed in the United States of America

ISBN 978-0-9969150-3-8   Hardcover Edition
ISBN 978-0-9969150-4-5   Softcover Edition

First Edition

16/1

"Get me my weapon." ~Padre Pio, referring to the Rosary

To my father, Russ, whose deep devotion to the Queen of Heaven he credits for his conversion from Protestantism to the Catholic faith in 1957.

CONTENTS

ACKNOWLEDGMENTS

The efforts of various crew at the apostolate of Church Militant / St. Michael's Media need to be acknowledged. Julie Muir has labored painstakingly over the look of the book, from its design and cover even to its feel. She always strives to make everything she does perfect, and this book is a prime example. Rodney Pelletier deserves praise for his tireless work at layout—meticulous work that can be challenging owing to the constant checking and shifting around of text and rechecking. He not only excelled at the layout, he also accomplished it in a speedy fashion. Christine Niles has earned high praise for her work at copy editing the original manuscript, which, given my "hunt and peck" typing style, created multiple typographical errors that needed to be fixed. She too is a perfectionist with her work and applies the same professionalism she brings to work to this book. And finally, Russ Voris, my dad, deserves acknowledgment for continually encouraging me to complete *The Weapon*. He kept reading bits and pieces and told me to just knuckle down and get it done—pretty much doing what a good dad does.

FOREWORD

The Rosary is a true means of hope, an avenue to hope, because it focuses our attention on the cause of our hope.

> But if Our Lord took the worst the world had to offer, and then by the power of God rose above it; if He, the unarmed, could make war with no other weapon other than goodness and pardon, so that the slain had the gain, and they who killed Him lost the day, then who should ever be without hope? Who shall ever despair in any momentary defeat by evil? Who shall fail to trust when he sees walking in the darkness the Risen One with glorious scars on hands and feet and side? The law He gave was clear: Life is a struggle; unless there is a Cross in our lives, there will never be an empty tomb; unless there is the crown of thorns, there will never be the halo of light; unless there is a Good Friday, there will never be an Easter Sunday. When He said: "I have conquered the world," He did not mean His followers would be immune from woes, pain, sorrow, and crucifixion. He gave no peace which promised a banishment from strife; for God hates peace in those who are destined for war. If the Heavenly Father did not spare His Son, He, the Heavenly Son, would not spare His disciples. What the Resurrection offered was not immunity from evil in the physical world, but immunity from sin in the soul. . . .

> No talisman was He to promise as security from trials; rather as a Captain He went into battle in order to inspire men to transfigure some of life's greatest pains into the richest gains of the spiritual

life. It was the Cross of Christ that raised the questions of life. It was the Resurrection that answered them. Not the feminine but the virile Christ is He Who unfurls before an evil world the pledge of victory in His own Body—the scar-spangled banner of Salvation. (*Life of Christ*, Ven. Abp. Fulton J. Sheen)

Because the Rosary focuses us on the very acts of salvation history, the war in which we are now each individually engaged until our last breath, it is a weapon, a spiritual weapon, with great power in the world of spiritual warfare, in otherworldly combat. It demands self-discipline and intensity of focus. The object of the focus is the very same kinds of combat and conflict that accompanied Our Lord throughout His life. Do not think there was no conflict present on Easter Sunday, for example; there certainly was. It was a combat between faith and nonfaith.

Combat and conflict, the sword was present at every step of Our Blessed Lord's earthly mission—every town He entered, every person He contacted, every cure He performed. Even for His Blessed Mother there was the trial of Her having to relinquish sole claim to Him and give Him to the world at the wedding of Cana. He brought this truth to Her when He said His hour had not yet come. There is no follower of Christ who does not engage in combat; it is not possible to follow Him and not at times be engulfed in struggle.

This is why the Rosary is so effective. It brings right to the front of our minds the need to be a fighter because we meditate on the reality of that truth in the life of Our Lord. He came to fight, to win, to save. We must do the same.

Catholics must recapture the militancy of the Faith, both internally and externally, but most especially internally. We have become soft in the soul, forgetting the intensity of spiritual combat and the need always to fight. We have misplaced the admonition of St. Paul, applied to himself, that he had fought the good fight—and without the good fight, there is no salvation. As the Ven. Abp. Fulton Sheen said in his book *Life of Christ*, "Without a Good Friday, there can be no Easter Sunday."

The Rosary is the weapon, the means to train soldiers in the Church Militant because its focus is the war on Hell. It is at the same time both an assault weapon and a defensive weapon. It guards your soul while it also launches crippling attacks against the demons. Demons are especially vulnerable to this weapon because it recalls to their intellects the very path trod by Christ to crush them underfoot. Their defeat is always before their eyes when you pray the Rosary.

Each "Hail Mary" is a deafening volley, each "Our Father," every "Glory Be" echoes off the caverns of Hell as they hear over and over again, "It is finished."

They are forever reminded of the path to Golgotha Our Lord walked, which began in Bethlehem, and even earlier in Nazareth. For millennia they sat in crazed fear, searched in vain for the Woman Who would crush their master's head. All of this is brought to their consciousness, their memories made present to their terrors, as they hear over and over the recounting of the war they have lost, battle by battle, pain by pain.

Take up your weapon and become stronger. Do not worry about fatigue, distraction, boredom, mental anxiety. Just pray. Pray to be better at prayer. Dwell on Our Lord's loneliness, His victory, and consider all of salvation history, for fifteen minutes, every day.

PROLOGUE

Mary! The very name of the Mother of God is a source of agony for the infernal regions. Demons hate Her! She is the path of grace, the path grace chose into the world—the avenue by which God Most High chose to enter into our frail existence. It was from this Woman that He took His Humanity. It was She, wrapped in mystery, Whom the legions of demons could not comprehend when the Most High foretold them of Her role in salvation history. They were confounded at the announcement.

It had, after all, been a woman that their master had chosen to initiate the downfall of humanity. It was Satan who had chosen the weapon, so it was God Who therefore would ratify that evil choice, turn it inside out and arrive on the field of battle with the Supreme Woman as His own weapon.

Catholic piety for many centuries has placed great emphasis on the tenderness of Mary, and deservingly so. She is Mother most pure, Mother most perfect. To Her children, She is the exemplar of tenderness and sweetness, for She rightfully is all these things by divine decree. To acknowledge this is to acknowledge and celebrate the will of the Most High. (And to deny it or ignore it, as Protestantism does, is spiritual folly.)

But to the legions of Hell, She is something entirely different. She is the Woman of Genesis, the Woman of the Apocalypse. And She is the greatest terror of the serpent. In Eden, the diabolical legions could not know they had already achieved their high-water mark, their most supreme victory. As the sun set that first night following the Fall of mankind, a new day was in the offing, a slow, constant march of rolling back from their victory. What would appear at the dawn would be a New Woman, a New Eve, Who comes forth brilliant as the dawn, terrible as an army arrayed for battle (Song of Sol. vi:10).

They had been allowed their hour, as they would be once more in another Garden, but from now on, the call of Heaven had gone out announcing the defeat of Hell—and at the head of the heavenly armies would be a Woman. They may have achieved their victory, but they would not be allowed to secure it. They had invaded, but they would not occupy and secure it as their own.

After Eden, Hell searched in vain for the Woman, looking, wondering precisely what the Most High could have meant by the prophetic decree that it would be a Woman who would crush the head of their lord.

This was a great confounding for the pride-swollen intellects of the damned angels. Mankind had fallen by their temptation. It was precisely their attack on a woman that had set in motion their victory over the object of their envy: humans. How could it now be that a Woman would rise up and deliver them a fatal blow? What their pride would not allow them to comprehend was the depth of the love the Most High held for His human creatures.

It has, in fact, been a continuing wonder even for us humans: What is man that you should care for him, mortal man that you should keep him in mind? (Ps. viii:4). And again, how can I repay the Lord for His goodness to me? (Ps. cxvi:12). And if we concentrate on the question, we will quickly realize that this will be the one question we will never have answered for us in eternity: Why, Heavenly Father, do You love me so much?

The depth of the intensity (notice the expression) of love for His human creatures was, in fact, the cause of the great envy on the part of the angels. Seeing His greater love for us than for them, they rejected His summons of service and rebelled entirely. It is a concept largely lost on many these days: God loves some more than He loves others. This was true of humanity with regard to the angels, and it is true of Mary with regard to the human race. Since in the divine economy, human beings ultimately occupy a higher place than angelic beings, it must also be grasped that there even exists among human beings a stratosphere of "rank" in relation to God.

By height or rank, what we mean is nearness to God, closeness to God, which is another way of saying a resemblance to God. This is the very definition of holiness. Who could more resemble God than the Woman from Whom God chose His human resemblance? While retaining Her status as creature, Mary looks like God and She more closely resembles God than any other creature could. So when the demons encounter the Woman, it is a horror to them.

They behold the single most glorified creature in the entirety of creation. It is impossible for them to look on Her and not see God in all His creative splendor. But there is a double source of their agony, and this one even worse than the first. The glory of the Woman is irradiated through Her humility. It is to their everlasting shame that every time they encounter Her, they are brought back to the moment they chose a Woman to be their nemesis.

The very weapon they chose to defeat the human creatures is the one the Most High has chosen and permitted to defeat them. (Talk about being beat at your own game.) And for the demonic, to be defeated in such a direct attack whereby their own plans were turned against them is a pain rivaling their deprivation of beatitude. Rightfully, then, does Holy Mother Church comprehend the Queen of Heaven as the terror of demons, for it is She Who crushes the serpent's head.

Speaking in terms of the temporal, before God created anything, He knew Mary. She was with Him from the beginning as the model of all He could desire because Her desire would be Him. When He made man after His own image, the image He had in mind was Her, the One Who would bring forth Himself, bone of Her bone and flesh of Her flesh.

She would desire Him as no other creature, and He could desire no other creature as much as Her because of Her great longing for Him. This longing for Him She transmits to Her offspring. No wonder Our Blessed Lord from the throne of His Cross identified St. John as Her son. John was the one Apostle who desired to be so close to His Lord, so longed to be with Him—even in the horror of

His pain—that he approached the Cross and stood there, being the first to receive the heavenly maternity of Mary.

The gift from God of Mary to us is to bring us to Himself. Her role is to present Him to us. Whoever receives Her receives Him. Whoever rejects Her rejects Him. She is the star that brings the morning; and with the morning, the night vanishes. So Mary has a dual role: the bringing of light and the conquest of darkness—but both roles are accomplished in the same reality.

While the Holy Rosary is correctly understood to be the prayer of Mary, it is the prayer that most exemplifies this dual aspect of Her blessed reality: bringer of light and vanquisher of darkness. She is the One in Whom the light rejoices and the One in Whom the darkness feels the thralls of terror.

This is why the Rosary is such a powerful weapon in the arsenal of spiritual warfare—it accomplishes each of these goals of bringing light that, by definition, dispels darkness. The one who grows in the Rosary, as the saints attest, will never be absent divine consolation.

A warning, however, must accompany the recitation of the Rosary, just as a great caution is issued when handling a deadly weapon. It must be appreciated for what it is: a weapon of great force intended to kill—to kill the night and liberate the light in our souls so that the stored-up light of grace and knowledge may flood our interior lives and fashion us into the divine militia.

The Rosary, coming from the hand of the Queen of Heaven, meant to make us concentrate on Her Son, to reflect on Him Who created Her, is the devotion the demons most fear. It can be properly spoken of as the fruit of union of the Flesh of Our Lord and His Mother, given to us by Her, about Him.

But we cannot forget the entire reason for this union in the first place was to do combat against the serpent, to crush him utterly. Therefore, the vision of the Rosary, the purely pietistic approach, is insufficient. It is a weapon of spiritual combat, replete with meditations on combat, about combat, for combat. It is meant to train up soldiers for combat—for the entire life of the Church Militant is all about combat, conflict, confrontation, and challenge.

The only comfort and consolation we are meant to draw is from the battlefield, not for its own sake, but for the sake of souls. We fight so we and others may live. The combat had produced a terrifying defeat for the sons of Man. The end of life in Eden was a frightening, crushing obliteration of how Adam and Eve had originally been created. From that point forward, the thorns would always be present. Life would be a scraping by, a drudgery, a series of almost hopeless moments stretching back to the memory of Eden. Man was enslaved.

But to one race, one nation, which God Himself brought forth, He promised liberation from the oppressor. There would be Good News; the sun would rise one day. There would be a new battle engaged, a war of such intensity, of such powerful force that the enemy could not begin to comprehend the level of defeat to which he and his legions would be subject.

A clock was now ticking. He had been warned, promised that his reign would not be everlasting, that an attack so ferocious was coming he would never recover from it. And it all began, this counteroffensive, in a small town 2,000 years ago, with an announcing—an annunciation—to a young Woman Whom Hell had completely overlooked.

INTRODUCTION

"The Mother of God contained the infinite God under Her heart, the God Whom no space can contain. Through Her, the Trinity is adored, demons are vanquished, Satan is cast out of Heaven, and our fallen nature is assumed into Heaven." ~St. Cyril of Alexandria

The Rosary may be the hardest daily devotional discipline ever presented to mankind. It can be dry, difficult for us to maintain concentration throughout its prayers, open to all kinds of distractions, easily given up on because of its challenges, and even an aid to insomnia from time to time. But all that is its precise point of strength. It's like Navy Seal training, preparation for an elite fighting force.

One particular difficulty I experience, in addition to those above, was finding an image to hang on to, to cultivate in my imagination while praying and meditating on the fourth and fifth Glorious Mysteries: the Assumption and the Coronation.

I could not find an immediate reference point in Scripture I could hold on to long enough to drive away distractions in my imagination. While meditating, for example, on the Scourging at the Pillar, there is ample visual scriptural imagery to so fill the mind I could at least offer some challenge to the usual distractions.

But it had always proven such a difficulty to overcome those challenges while praying the last two Glorious Mysteries that it felt like a drudgery to pray the Rosary on Wednesdays and Sundays. You want to pray well, and when you don't, it can easily become discouraging and frustrating. And of course, with two days a week being unsettling, the pattern for the rest of the week also became unsettled.

The tugs of time and constant activity create a juxtaposition to the reciting the Rosary. The very thing the Rosary helps to contend with is the same thing that makes the saying of the Rosary difficult: distractions.

So, aware of the difficulty of distraction coupled with the inability to successfully meditate on the fourth and fifth Glorious Mysteries, one day I asked my Heavenly Mother if She would help me get over this. What could I successfully meditate on while praying the decade dedicated to Her Assumption?

On a trip to Australia for a speaking engagement in 2012, I was praying Morning Prayer. The particular psalm was Psalm 16. And then like a bolt of lightning there it was, in almost the final verse: "For thou dost not give me up to Sheol, or let thy godly one see the Pit" (Ps. xvi:10).

A spiritual Eureka moment, praise God. Thank you, Blessed Mother. I realized immediately two things: One, I was dumb for not having seen it much earlier; two, the whole psalm, while obviously focused on Our Lord, is by extension focused on all those conformed to Him, and since no one is more conformed to Him than His own Mother, of course this applied to Her as well.

Then I went back up to the beginning of the psalm and re-read it and saw the Mother of God all over it. From the opening line—"Preserve me, O God, for in thee I take refuge" (Ps. xvi:1)—She is the Mother of refuge. "As for the saints in the land, they are the noble, in whom is all my delight" (Ps. xvi:3). How true for the Mother of God, for She is our Mother as well, given to us from the Cross —and She does delight in us.

As I read further, the pointings to the Blessed Mother became ridiculously apparent. All throughout every stanza, there was Mary.

But one stanza, besides the obvious one of Her not undergoing corruption, stood out extremely clearly. It pointed to Her purity, Her singlemindedness, the complete and total gift of Herself: "Those who choose another god multiply their sorrows; their libations of blood I will not pour out or take their names upon my lips" (Ps. xvi:4).

This immediately shows forth combat, rival, challenge, contest. Even for the Mother of God there is contest, for She is in contest with the Ancient Enemy for the souls of Her children, Her offspring. And She directs Her offspring against his offspring. This is carved deeply into the decades of the Holy Rosary, for it is a complete meditation on the struggle, the combat, the very heart of the work of the Church Militant.

Venerable Abp. Fulton Sheen had, among other things, this to say about the Rosary:

> The Rosary is the book of the blind, where souls see and there enact the greatest drama of love the world has ever known; it is the book of the simple, which initiates them into mysteries and knowledge more satisfying than the education of other men; it is the book of the aged, whose eyes close upon the shadow of this world, and open on the substance of the next. The power of the Rosary is beyond description. (*The World's First Love*)

The Rosary is both training for spiritual war and its execution all at the same moment; for the moment one begins to pray it, its spiritual effects begin.

The soul increases in might, spiritual might, first to be able to ward off the enemy and secondly to eventually master him. It is a meditation on the Savior, the life of the Savior, from the announcement of His birth until the final realization of His work—the coronation of the Virgin Mary as Queen of Heaven and Earth and of the entire universe. *to proclaim the Kingdom of God*

He came to save. Period. And who is more spectacularly saved than His own Mother? In Her, all the saved are represented, for She is the new Mother of all the living. But the saved are saved through battle, spiritual combat. There is no other way to Heaven—it must be fought for, and a fighter needs training and self-discipline.

Spiritual combat is not for the faint of heart; it is, in fact, how the

Catholic life is lived. It is the daily call of duty; this is why there is daily prayer. Pope Leo XIII's insight is just as true today as it was when he first wrote near the close of the 19th century: "[Catholics] are born for combat." The combat we enter into is control of ourselves and over the temptings of the enemy. We begin wounded by sin from our con-ception. Baptism removes the sin, but the temporal effects of the sin, concupiscence, remains.

Concupiscence is that quality—since it originates from sin—that makes sin attractive to us. Concupiscence knows its mother was Original Sin and is always seeking her out. The will ordered to disobedience, the intellect obscured, these become the weapons of fallen nature to rebel against God and seek our own pleasure.

Such a powerful weapon available to the enemy needs a superior weapon to overwhelm it. In the history of warfare, the side with the best weaponry and arsenal is the side that prevails. The same is true in the spiritual war. The Rosary is the superior weapon against concupiscence because of the discipline it demands to achieve faithful repetition; because of the mental energy required to concentrate on its mysterious depths; because of the ordering of life to ensure time to pray it.

In the actual praying of the Rosary, these goals are being achieved, however imperfectly, incompletely, or haltingly. An earthly army does not move at a precise pace each day; it does not conquer the same amount of land each day. Each battle does not present the same degree of intensity. Some battles are much more intense, others less so, but they are each battles nonetheless. Some days are easier for the soldier, and some more difficult. For the soldier, the great unknown is: What will this day bring?

Training for war is a process. It requires time, patience, and work. The same is true of spiritual war. Each requires the self-mastery sorely needed to "man up" and protect that which we are called to defend, namely, our souls, and to the extent that we can help others, their souls as well.

While it would not seem the case, given the current culture in the

Church, the Rosary is a prayer men specifically should pick up. It is our hope, in fact, that this book will inspire more men to see and consider the very masculine nature of the Rosary. Its purpose is to perfect those who pray it, to become fighters and warriors, but it has the common perception of being a "woman" thing, something associated with the feminine. There are obvious connections to the feminine, since it is a prayer dedicated to and given us from the Queen of Heaven. But while we are still on this earth, Her Royalty directs us to fight—She is Queen of a heavenly army, the Church Militant, and to fail to understand this is to relegate Her queenship to a nostalgic piety rather than see it as an active spiritual force overwhelming the forces of Satan.

Every "Hail Mary" uttered with any level of thought is a bullet straight to the pride of Satan because it reminds him of the beginning of his undoing, the very words spoken by his former comrade, Gabriel, to the Queen, and then from the mouth of the mother of John the Baptist, who would prepare the world for Christ's coming, heralding the eventual end of Satan's reign.

And then there is the prayer to protect us and pray for us not just now, but at the moment of death—that moment when his final assault will be most vicious because it will be his last attempt, and he knows it. Failing the conquest of the faithful at that moment, we, formerly lost to him, enter into the everlasting protection and joy of our heavenly Mother.

This is war. The sword will never depart from our house while we still breathe. This necessitates our being the most complete soldiers, fighters, warriors we can be. There is nothing "girly" or "sissy" about the Rosary or about those who pray it. On the contrary, what is "girly" is to fail to pray it, to shy away from it, because it demands a call to duty not to be overwhelmed on the spiritual battlefield.

The fight may be exhausting at times, but there is nothing like the taste of victory. Pain is temporary; victory is forever. Every soldier knows this, and the good ones always keep this in the forefront of their minds. Defeat is not an option. Conquest, total defeat, and overrunning of the enemy is the goal, and hence the motivation. But we must keep secure in the conflict; we must fight with a relentlessness the enemy cannot match.

We must fight harder, be more intense, attack more often than the enemy. Bear in mind that while he is a spiritual being, we have spiritual beings fighting for us as well. The Rosary is a call to arms for them, a trumpet blast from us, beseiged by the enemy, to send in the cavalry, to bring up reinforcements, and to summon our terrible twelve-star general to the front lines to crush his head, as a prelude to the final crushing that all humanity—saved and damned, all Heaven and Hell—will witness on the Last Day.

So with the militaristic understanding of the Rosary planted in our consciousness, let us proceed to examine and reflect on each of the mysteries from the point of view of combat, conflict, contradiction, and challenge, for one or more is present in each mystery.

Chapter 1

THE FIRST JOYFUL MYSTERY:

The Annunciation

After centuries and centuries of waiting, Heaven's sneak attack into enemy territory is launched. It's akin to being dropped behind enemy lines. In the womb of the most humble of all humans ever to live, God takes on flesh, incarnates, with the eventual goal of bringing redemption to all mankind and extending the effect of that redemption down through the ages in His Mystical Body, the Catholic Church.

That redemption will be wrought by destroying the kingdom that currently rules the earth. This incarnate God is King, and in both His physical body and His Mystical Body—the Catholic Church —He will fight and defeat the prince of this world (as He will refer to him in later years).

(There is a reason that so much of world literature is dominated by this particular theme—Richard the Lion-Hearted, for example, returning secretly to England to overthrow his wicked brother Prince John, who had set up his own throne. Even something as recent as *Star Wars* depends on the theme of the authentic rulers stealthily overthrowing the usurpers of power.)

But now that God has entered time, He will proceed in time. Before the Mystical Body can be fully realized, the fleshly body must first be conceived, grow, be nurtured and come to full maturity. The Annunciation can just as easily be called the Incarnation, for that is the end, the reason for Gabriel's announcing to Mary Her special, unique, singular place of honor in the mind and heart of Heaven. This moment is the moment for which all humanity was prepared from the Fall in the Garden when the Father declared to the serpent, "I will put enmity between you and the woman, and between your seed and her seed" (Gen. iii:15).

1

Church tradition holds that before material creation, Almighty God had revealed to the angelic realm He would create a physical realm and populate it with not merely material life, but with mate-rial life that would be ensouled, and this ensouled flesh would be man.

And unlike the life of angelic beings, man's life would proceed in a chain of successive moments called time. Man would generate life from his own life, participate in the very cre-ative power of God, a power not granted to superior beings of the universe. Man would possess the power to procreate, to bring forth future citizens of Heaven. The power of procreation, because it was a power proper to the nature of man and not to angelic beings, would thus become a major target of the diabolical as human history advanced.

Man, lacking in intellect compared to the angels, would have to "catch up" to a point in history when the demonic could launch an effective assault on this procreative power. The trap had been laid down the road, so to speak. All that remained was for mankind eventually to fall in. Only time would be needed for the great power man had been given to be completely perverted by a dia-bolical assault. That assault began wholesale in the 20th century with the introduction of widespread birth control, more rightly understood and called conception prevention—or its more com-monly used name, contraception, i.e., "against conception."

How infuriated Satan must have been when his intellect grasped the notion that God had become Immanuel ("God with us") through the very power He had denied the angels, and one of the causes of their rebellion. It can be no wonder that in introducing the contraceptive mindset to contemporary man, he must have been accomplishing two missions: limiting the number of humans, and getting "revenge" on God.

In trying to limit the number of humans, consider that Satan gets no joy from those who are damned. In tempting souls into Hell, he is merely following the call of his now perverted angelic nature. There is no recompense, no reward, no feeling of satisfaction for him as the damned fall into Hell.

There is, however, a searing pain he experiences at each and every soul saved. Those souls are an everlasting shame for him because they are now forever out of his reach—and not only out of his reach, but now behold for everlasting what he will never behold —the life of the Blessed Trinity.

The elect will see God in the face, the Beatific Vision; and this will be an everlasting torment to Satan, to the one who wanted all humanity to be denied its end, and who now must contend with the reality that his plans are foiled—some of humanity *will* be saved, forever and ever, world without end.

On a minimal level, it can be compared to a great coach who has won championships and established an incredible record in the process. He wins almost every competition he engages in—almost every competition. Almost.

Whenever these great coaches are interviewed, coaches like Notre Dame head coach Lou Holtz, you will inevitably hear them say that their most vivid memories are not of the wins, however stunning and brilliant they may have been, but of the losses.

The pain of the loss stings them until they go to the grave, and can never be erased from their minds. No matter how many games, comeback victories, national championships they were a part of, those games lost are forever etched in their psyches. They can never be replayed, never won again, the loss never reversed, forever and ever, world without end. They are in the history books, and the books are closed. Period.

It is impossible for us mortals to consider the agony this brings to Satan—that there are souls he will never be able to tempt into sin, to torture in Hell forever. Every soul that escapes him is "the one that got away."

It is of no consequence to him that the vast majority of humanity is damned, as the saints, martyrs, mystics, popes, Fathers, and Doctors of the Church have restated for 2,000 years. What is of consequence to him are the ones who escape him, despite their being few in number in relation to the rest of the race.

So Satan has no desire to see humanity keep multiplying. He hates everything human, especially this power that cooperates and associates itself so much with the divine power of creation. So every new human conceived has a double pain for him: that the new human is a continuing reference point of God's abiding love for humanity, which surpasses that of His love for the angels, for He did not join their nature to Himself; and with each new conception, the threat has now materialized that another soul may escape Satan. His hatred of humanity is desperate and wild because each new person is an agony of despair for him, for he knows that some of the new souls created this day will escape him, however few they may be.

That the Almighty would deign to take on the material flesh of what Satan considered a lesser creature was unanticipated, completely beyond what his pride could imagine. It was a bafflement to him. How could God love this creature raised from the slime of the earth so totally and completely as to join them to Himself? It is not only mankind in Heaven that will always wonder at this, but the damned as well: Why does God so love humanity?

The announcement to the legions of angels that this would be the "future" caused war to break out among them. God communicated to them that He would join Himself to this race, clothe Himself in flesh so He could be present completely to them in their existence.

And then came the announcement that thundered throughout the angelic world: In all their created glory and splendor, they would worship their Creator not just as He was present to them currently, in spirit, but also as He would be present to them in the flesh—and not just flesh alone, but in flesh He would draw directly from them. He would be born of woman.

Vast numbers of angelic beings revolted against this divine revelation, led by one of the most glorious creatures ever brought into creation—Lucifer. And thus began the great rebellion, the cosmological clash that continues unabated to this day. They would not worship flesh, even if that flesh was joined to the Divine Majesty in some mysterious fashion beyond their comprehension. They would not worship it.

They rebelled and consequently were deprived of any future hope of being admitted to the Beatific Vision. They had never and would never see God in the face. So refused admittance by their own choice, God prepared a place less painful for them than constantly beholding His magnificent beauty, which to them would be a source of unendurable agony—for in their rebellion, they had become hideous creatures of darkness and ugliness.

So they fell from the angelic realm like lightning to the realm of no hope. They could not brook the kingdom of beauty, so in His mercy God provided for them the kingdom of despair and regret, the horrors and tortures of which could not compare to the agony of suffering they would experience if He had commanded them to remain in the presence of His divine glory. The fire of His holiness would have been infinitely more painful to them than the fires of Hell, their new and abiding home.

But they went to Hell armed with the knowledge God had given them: that He would become flesh and would be born of a Woman. So when material creation flowed from the Divine Majesty and man was formed and came into being in the divine image, the agents of rebellion, intent on revenge, set about to thoroughly corrupt the divine plan. If God so loved man, then man would be the object of their infernal hatred. They could not touch God, but they could touch those He loved.

It is not coincidence that Lucifer approached the woman with his malfeasance. And when Eve was duped and fell from grace, bringing her husband with her into her sin, Satan rejoiced in his evil. Having the singular place in creation of not only realizing the full effect of sin but also being its author, he knew God could not join Himself to sin. In his corrupted intellect, he thought he had won. Man became mortal and fell from grace, just as Lucifer had. For all the revelations of God and their magnificence, he had defeated the Most High—or so he imagined.

5

It was at this moment, what he thought was his supreme victory, that God revealed to him his error.

Eve, this woman, was not *the Woman*. There would be another, and this one Satan would not overwhelm. Her he would not even touch, in any fashion. As he occupied a singular role in creation, so would She.

In this great rebellion, Satan, the serpent, had chosen the weapon —woman. So the Almighty, having granted Satan the choice, would now fight back with the same weapon. She would be the instrument by which his rebellion would at last be crushed underfoot. The Woman of the Genesis prophecy would bring God into the world, would bring redemption, salvation, and ultimate victory for Heaven and defeat for Hell.

The utter and total defeat Satan had tasted in a lightning flash in the spiritual realm he would now be made to drink the fullness of in the earthly realm. God would be born of Woman, and in so coming forth from Her, She would be the instrument by which his head would be crushed. Enmity, everlasting hatred, would be placed between Her and him. All that needed to be done was wait. So the powers of Hell waited and searched and plundered human existence at every turn, every new human being, desperately seeking after the Woman and Her offspring who would be their ultimate defeat.

Millennia later, the angel Gabriel was sent by God to a Virgin in the town of Nazareth betrothed to a man named Joseph, who was of the house of David, and the Virgin's name was Mary. His message to Her from the heavenly realms: You will conceive and bear a Son.

The sneak attack had been launched. The undoing of the prince of this world had been set in motion without his even being aware of it.

In war, a fifth column—a military reference to enemy troops behind the lines—is often instrumental in securing victory. Fifth columns disrupt enemy communications, sabotage supply lines, work to create chaos and fear and neuter the enemy's ability to wage an effective defense. Part of the strategy, however, includes by necessity actually getting behind enemy lines and then securing sufficient cover to proceed undetected. Many spy novels and film plots revolve around this theme.

The Incarnation was a fifth column move. Never in history was there as perfectly executed a strategy to get behind enemy lines and move about undetected. There was the silent invasion into the womb of Mary—unseen by the enemy. But it was not just the transport of Heaven into its fleshy dwelling that escaped Hell's notice; it was also the specific fleshy dwelling that provided the perfect hiding place.

The creature of highest pride could have nothing to do with such a lowly creature as a humble virgin girl in a small backwater town. It's not altogether clear such a creature would have even appeared on his radar, to use more contemporary wording. But we do know he was hunting, yet his pride prevented him from reasoning as God. Those who are closely conformed to God have some access to the divine mind, His divine actions. As they draw closer to God by uniting themselves to His divine will, they necessarily partake in His divine mind, His wisdom. So, too, the opposite is true. Those who are least conformed to the divine will have least access to the divine mind, so Satan would have struggled even to conceive that the divine treasure would invade his territory, his kingdom, his realm, cloaked in the seeming poverty of a young girl from nowhere.

But as we peer into the account of the Incarnation, we find a struggle even within the mind of Our Blessed Mother, moments before She actually becomes Our Blessed Mother. When Gabriel greeted Her with the salutation that could only apply to Her, Mary was disturbed. She was disturbed at his words and wondered what kind of greeting this might be. He had greeted Her with the salutation "Hail," an honorific title. Here was a messenger of Heaven giving Her honor. In Her true humility, She could not fathom why She should be greeted this way—especially by an angelic being, who may have been the first creature in all creation to be given the news, to run "recon" behind enemy lines and deliver the dispatch that the General would soon be arriving.

She was shaken, disturbed. Humility does not easily comprehend being honored. And in the case of Our Lady, there would immediately follow another revelation that gave Her great pause owing to Her great humility. After hearing the heavenly consolation—"Do not be afraid, Mary, for you have found favor with God" (Luke i:30)—there instantly came the heavenly dispatch that She was the Woman of Genesis prophecy. "[S]he will bear a son, and you shall call his name Jesus, for he will save his people from their sins" (Matt. i:21).

Mary of Nazareth had never intended to have a child. She had promised Her virginity to God. The times into which Mary had been born were intensely expectant of the birth of the Messiah, the liberator of Israel. Any woman capable of conceiving would have been desirous of being the mother of the Messiah. No doubt, some were even beseeching Heaven to be so honored.

Yet so humble was She, this young Virgin, that She had decided to exclude Herself from any such blessing from Heaven. Mary had decided long before that She would offer Heaven Her virginity so as not to be the Messiah's Mother. This much is clear from Her immediate response to Gabriel, that She was preserving Her virginity for life. "How shall this be, since I have no husband?" (Luke i:34).

She was not challenging Gabriel like Zechariah had at the announcement of John the Baptist's conception. She was, rather, lost in contemplation and wonder. Stirring deep inside Her was a realization that all this was true, but it still had to be reconciled with the natural order. She understood the spernatural marvel, but wondered at its completion in Her.

And then the intimacy of the inner life of the divinity was revealed to Her. The Holy Spirit, Her Spouse, was presented to Her and the will of Her Father would overshadow Her; She would be led into the court of the King because He so desired Her beauty. And the Son of God would be Her Son as well.

And to alleviate any further wonder in Her mind, to raise wonder to the level of marvel—"And behold, your kinswoman Elizabeth in her old age has also conceived a son; and this is the sixth month with her who was called barren. For with God nothing will be impossible" (Luke i:34). And there She had it: Nothing was impossible for God.

"[L]et it be to me according to your word" (Luke i:38). And accordingly God leapt from Heaven into time, laying aside His divine glory and taking on the created glory of His creation. He brought Himself in His totality to the womb of Mary—His divinity—and united it to His fleshly created Body and Blood and Soul. He had been given His orders, sent out a recon unit, delivered the dispatch, communicated the plan, donned the disguise, and set the plan in motion.

The most glorious war was now prepared to be launched. At the end of that war, He would let rip the victory cry from the Cross: "It is finished." This quiet evening, in Nazareth, away from the gaze and ears of all humanity, and most importantly the enemy, He lay quietly and still in the womb and said secretly to His Mother, "It has begun."

Chapter 2

THE SECOND JOYFUL MYSTERY:

The Visitation

History records for us that at the time of Our Lord's conception and birth, there had been a great expectation of the coming of the Messiah. This may have been due in large part to the desire of the Jews to see the overthrow of their Roman overlords. It may also have been a stirring of the Holy Spirit to encourage a great hope in the hearts of men. In fact, it would not have been the case without a prompting of Heaven, for Heaven can certainly use the conditions of fallen man to effect a good.

And it would be a good, because it would be most fitting for God to become incarnate in a season of hope. They, the Chosen People of God, were living under the foot of the most powerful ruler in the history of the world: Caesar. His forces occupying their land were cruel and taxed them heavily. So there was a great desire for liberation—in fact, more than a desire, but an actual, tangible hope, an expectation, an awaiting. But what they missed was that the spiritual oppression from which they were suffering had even greater need of being liberated from. Even crueler than the emperor in Rome was the prince of this world. This is the one from whom they needed true liberation.

Nonetheless, they longed for a new David, and any woman of the day who could bear children desired to be the mother of the new David. The mother of the new king had a dual honor. The women all understood they would not only be the instrument God would use to usher in liberation from the oppressor, but in keeping with royal custom in the Davidic realm, she would also be queen, for it was not the wife but the mother of the king who was queen.

The women, therefore, of early first-century Israel each longed to be chosen by Heaven for this magnificent honor—all except one.

There was among them one so deep in humility, so deep in self-understanding in relation to the Almighty, that She not only considered Herself the lowliest of creatures, unfit to be the mother of the Messiah, that She took active steps to remove Herself from consideration. She would never know man. She would keep Her virginity out of humility. She would thus ensure that She could never be the Mother of the Messiah because She would never be able to conceive Him in Her womb.

It was first Her humility and then Her pledged virginity that had been the source of Her confusion and disturbance at the words of Gabriel. That the Almighty would send a messenger to Her and announce that She had found favor with Heaven, that She was full of grace, caused Her great disturbance. How could this be? She was unworthy.

But She did not utter that aloud. Then the angel announced to Her something far greater—that She would be the Mother of not only the Messiah, but the Mother of the Messiah Who was also the Son of the Most High. She would be the Mother of the Lord.

On this score, She was no longer able to ponder over Her confusion as She had at the greeting that She was full of grace. That greeting could play over silently in Her mind. This announcement could not stay silent in Her heart. She had to speak. "How shall this be, since I have no husband?" (Luke i:34). (The Holy Spirit would come upon Her and the power of the Most High would overshadow Her.)

Without complete understanding, but with complete trust born from Her humility, She consented—and God mingled His divinity with humanity in Her most blessed womb. The Woman of the prophecy of Genesis was now revealed.

It was the Trinity that had condemned the serpent in the Garden, and now for the first time in history, the Holy Trinity made itself blindingly clear: The Third Person came upon Her, the First Person overshadowed Her, and the Second Person appeared in flesh within Her.

At this moment, She now understood. She knew on a level no other human could know (unless that other human had been sufficiently enlightened by the Holy Spirit as well). Gabriel had said to Mary that nothing was impossible with God, and as a sign, Mary's kinswoman Elizabeth, deprived of children and well into old age, had conceived a son as well.

Exploding with excitement and desiring to behold the glory of God, Mary not only set out for the hill country where Elizabeth and her husband Zechariah lived, but she set out in haste. Such should always be the response of the Church Militant, the Church on earth still fighting evil—to respond with joy, to rush into battle, to see the glory of God made manifest in material creation.

Elizabeth, in her sixth month of pregnancy, had no idea of what had happened to Mary in Nazareth just days before. But all it took was the sound of Mary's voice for the child in her womb to be baptized and for the Holy Spirit to fill her as well. The kinswoman of Mary would give birth to the second person in human history who would come into the world without original sin, for the sound of Mary's voice carried with it the Divine Presence in Her immaculate womb, and that Logos baptized John in Elizabeth's miraculous womb.

Already, the Woman of Genesis was being used to crush the enemy's head. While John the Baptist was conceived in original sin, as all humanity had been with the singular exception of Mary, at the sound of the voice of the Mother of God, his original sin was purged. He was conceived in the womb in sin, but he emerged from that same womb sinless. So intense and real was this grace that in the womb he leapt for joy—the joy that comes from intimate union with God.

And that joy cannot be contained. This moment of superabundant grace spilled over to his mother Elizabeth, who was filled with the Holy Spirit, as she stood in the presence of His Spouse. She gave voice not only for herself, but for the son leaping around inside her. "Blessed are you among women, and blessed is the fruit of your womb!" (Luke i:42).

All Mary had done was simply call out to her. They had no conversation up to that point—but none was needed. So much a living temple of God had Mary become, so much a living monstrance bringing Our Lord out to the world, that Elizabeth, filled with the Holy Spirit, immediately apprehended the truth. "And why is this granted me, that the mother of my Lord should come to me?" (Luke i:43).

Elizabeth is blessed to become the first person in history to recognize, fully and completely standing before her, the Woman of Genesis—the Queen. Her own son would become, by Heaven's desire, the herald of the new King. He would be the instrument by which God would declare war aloud on Satan and his kingdom of rebel demons.

This is why John would emerge from the womb unstained by sin; he was the trumpet, and the trumpet needed to be clear, untainted, able to give the clarion call so that no one could mistake it. This would be a fight to the death, and humanity was put on notice. Soon, two great armies would be foraging across the landscape of human history, one led by the rebellious prince, the other by the King of Heaven, with His own cousin being the first. Because of John the Baptist's unique role, Our Blessed Lord would later say of him, "I tell you, among those born of women none is greater than John" (Luke vii:28).

At the mere utterance of a greeting—the voice coming from the Queen of that great army—John was bursting with joy, and not only ready but prepared to engage in battle. In response to John's exaltation and Elizabeth's spirit-filled homage to Her, Mary responded with Her own recognition of the coming battle and Her role in it. "For behold, henceforth all generations will call me blessed" (Luke i:48). "[H]e has scattered the proud in the imag-ination of their hearts, he has put down the mighty from their thrones, and exalted those of low degree" (Luke i:51–52).

It is through Her fiat that all this would be accomplished. The putting down of the mighty from their thrones is the natural outcome of the Almighty coming to the scene, for the mighty pale in comparison to Him Who is All Might.

Many years later, Mary's Son would say from the Cross to a young man named John, "Behold, your mother!" (John xix:27). But here at the beginning, Mary would spiritually adopt another John. Scripture makes the point that Mary was present at the birth of John the Baptist by telling us: "And Mary remained with her about three months" (Luke i:56). She stayed with Elizabeth about three months, which is when John would have been born, since Elizabeth was already with child at six months when His Queen arrived at the home of his parents.

So at the very beginning of His life, present to Her, Her Divine Son gives Her a John for Her son. So too at the end of His life with Her, He would entrust another John to Her maternal love as yet another son. It is divinely fitting that it would be Mary Who would receive the conclusion of the Old Testament into Her immaculate hands as John emerged from the womb of Elizabeth. The former was now being received by the latter, the old into the new, the past into the future—and the bridge between was Mary.

All before had been preparation, arrangements, for this moment —all generations would call Her blessed because She was to be the bridge for eternity. As baby John the Baptist lay in Her hands at the moment of his birth, the Old and the New Testament met on the bridge of Mary. In Her hands lay the culmination of all prep-aration; under Her heart lay the fulfillment of all that had been prepared for. Three months earlier, this moment had been antici-pated by the Mother of God in Her Magnificat. "He has helped his servant Israel, in remembrance of his mercy, as he spoke to our fathers, to Abraham and to his posterity for ever." (Luke i:54–55).

Here in Her hands were the children of Abraham, the last and final prophet, the final sum-up of the people of the Old Covenant. Our Lord would say of him many years later, "I tell you, among those born of women none is greater than John" (Luke vii:28). And no woman had been greater than Mary. How beautiful an expression of divine arrangement was it that the greatest man ever born would be delivered from the womb into the hands of the greatest Woman ever born—two creatures of God, each free from Original Sin, born to bring war against the author of sin. The clouds of war were collecting on the horizon, gathering in thicker formation, but here in the house of Zechariah the battle plan was cast. King and Queen and herald were in holy conspiracy. The gathering clouds were an ominous warning to Hell.

Chapter 3

THE THIRD JOYFUL MYSTERY:

The Birth of Our Lord

Make no mistake—that little Babe, the small, shivering Christ Child, had come to kill. He came to declare war and vanquish an oppressed race. Lying there in poverty in a carved-out hole in the ground was the perfect disguise to keep the enemy's eyes from locating Him. The King at last makes His appearance, but He is wearing camouflage. He is known and recognized only by His closest allies—the Queen, His foster father, guardian and protector, some humble shepherds, and the Wise Men of the East.

The wise and humble always see through His disguise. The proud and stupid are always fooled. The angelic realm, of course, know Him, and draw the distinction between those who recognize Him and those who don't. Their message is in two parts. First is the announcement that He has been born and that this good news is "to all the people" (Luke ii:10). But then comes the rather ominous note that while the good news is for everyone, not everyone will accept the gift of peace being extended by Heaven. "[A]nd on earth peace among men with whom he is pleased!" (Luke ii:14).

And there it is. The King has arrived armed with the weapons of war to defeat the enemy, and yet there will be those who will side with the enemy, unable to accept Heaven's salvation because they are not of good will. It is of these His Father spoke when He said to the serpent that He too would have offspring—and that the hatred between the Woman and the serpent would extend to the offspring of both. "I will put enmity between you and the woman, and between your seed and her seed" (Gen. iii:15).

So here is the offspring of the Woman made visible, and already the clouds of war are gathering, proclaimed by the angels giving glory to God, trumpeting that the battle has ensued. Indeed, one of the offspring of the serpent is already making war on the allies of the Child of Heaven as he tries to trick them into revealing the location of the newborn King. Herod, under the control of the diabolical, was the first offspring of the serpent to try and attack the offspring of the Woman. He would not be the last.

As the shepherds come to the stable and retell the happenings that had just occurred on the hills as they sat in the nightwatch keeping guard over their flock, the Queen Mother listened intently. It was not the first time She had received a communication from the angelic realms, despite this one being relayed indirectly. One angel had told Her that Her Son would be set on the throne of David, that He would rule over the house of Jacob forever, that His kingdom would have no end.

Now come the shepherds bearing a confirmation of the presence of the Savior on earth that they had heard from an angel. "[F]or to you is born this day in the city of David a Savior, who is Christ the Lord" (Luke ii:11). He was not only the Messiah of Whom they had been told, but also God—exactly what Mary had been told nine months earlier in Nazareth and in the same type of communication. "He will be great, and will be called the Son of the Most High" (Luke i:32).

She had heard further confirmation from another earthly source whose insight was also evidently inspired by Heaven, owing to her own miraculous maternity. Elizabeth declared Mary to be "the mother of my Lord" (Luke i:43), which says more about Her Child than it does Her. Three times at least in nine months Mary had heard Her Child was divine. But only twice had She heard from others He would be the Savior. The third time She heard it was when it spilled over from Her own humility. "[A]nd my spirit rejoices in God my Savior" (Luke i:47).

Her Son, the fruit of Her immaculate womb, had come to save, to rescue. And if God Himself desired to come to earth to make war, then the enemy must indeed be a formidable one—all this as She sat in the stable, holding God, pondering and treasuring it in Her heart. She would soon hear the cost of bearing these things in Her heart. And the source again would be an emissary inspired by Heaven warning resolutely of the cost of this war.

What these meditations draw out is the reality of the situation, the war in which we are engaged. There is no retreat from this war. The battle ends when our life on earth ends. It begins almost immediately—as soon as our conscious minds are capable of knowing right from wrong. From that moment onward, we are in combat to reverse the effects of Original Sin, to try and restore within ourselves the order that existed before the Fall.

In the Fall, the prior reality was upended; no longer were our passions at the service of our intellects, but the order inverted. Try as we might, even the greatest men to follow after Eden could not do this, could not conquer. Abraham, Moses, David, the Prophets —none of them could overcome the reality of our defeated situation. They were like soldiers in a prisoner of war camp. They needed to be rescued, set free. But no one among men had the constitution to effect the escape. All their deficiencies, their weaknesses, their sins, had a cumulative effect, so there had to be One who could carry the accumulated weight of all sin and its effects. And since the sins of all were transmitted in and executed by the body, the One would have to have a body to bear the burden.

The burden borne in the divinely created humanity of Jesus was one capable of bearing in its flesh all the sins of mankind, and not in just some pietistical, poetic way, but in actual reality—all the pain, spiritual and physical, all the effects of all the sin of all the human race, were to be borne on the Cross in the flesh of that small Child currently in the manger.

The Wise Men knew this in a dim fashion, at least through some intuition or prompting from Heaven. They brought myrrh as a recognition, a foreshadowing, of His agony, to place at the crib of the King destined to die, for unlike those He would liberate, all born to live, He was born to die. The Divine Justice was embraced and swallowed whole in the Divine Mercy. This Child was a killer, a disease, a rebellion to the prince of this world.

Chapter 4

THE FOURTH JOYFUL MYSTERY:

The Presentation

The legal place among the Jews held by the firstborn male was one of extreme importance. It went to the heart of Jewish culture, so much so that a law reserved for just the firstborn male had been established by God specifically for the firstborn.

God had commanded that each firstborn male be presented to Him in a Temple offering. It was to take place forty days after birth, when the mother was past her time of ritual impurity. So it was that Joseph and Mary arrived at the Temple to do for Jesus what was prescribed by the law. But there was waiting for them in the Temple a man whose moment of death was being forestalled until the arrival of the Messiah.

His name was Simeon, and of him we do not know much, other than that he was a devout and upright man. It had been made known to him by the Holy Spirit he would not die until he had seen the Messiah with his own eyes. What we can safely assume is that Simeon must have been a man of deep holiness to be afforded such a singular grace. In addition to being devout and morally upright, there must have been a deep, abiding presence of faith and hope and charity. His canticle to God after he took the Babe into his arms speaks of this.

He knew intuitively of the great battle about to ensue. He knew it in his bones, his soul, his mind. He knew also that this was not just a battle involving his own race, but was a war involving all humanity. He knew the stakes were nothing less than salvation, and that this was for the nations. He knew too the cost of this Great War would be incalculable suffering. So when he returns the Babe to the arms of His Mother and father, he takes Mary aside and says to Her that She would suffer most of all—a sword would pierce Her immaculate soul.

The Son of God is barely a month old and already the sword makes its first appearance in His life, drawn against His Mother—a sign of the horror of sin. The most perfect human to have ever graced the earth would have to bear in Her soul the pain of sin, having never committed a single one in Her life, never even having been touched by Original Sin. To Her would be the utmost sharing of the future pain of Her Son.

This sword would appear again in His life on earth, drawn against Him in His infancy by Herod's soldiers. It would also bring forth the Church from His side on the Cross as it would be plunged into His dead body. But He Himself would also have a sword and would never hesitate to draw it and use it. He said, "I have not come to bring peace, but a sword" (Matt. x:34). And this is fitting, for there is no war without weapons. Weapons exist to be used, and more than used, to defeat, kill, conquer, vanquish, and occupy.

The sword of Christ is truth, and it hurts as it tears into the soul, separating sinew from bone; it hurts more than a physical sword. Rarely does a physical battle wound so change a man as to conform him to Heaven. Its ability to effect change is limited to the merely natural, the body. But the sword the Son of God never sheathes can so wound a man, so disfigure and kill a former man of sin, that a new man of justice can emerge, where God will lovingly give him what he deserves, and that will be Himself.

The target of the divine sword is sin, to cut out the gore and ugliness of it and repair and restore man. In this manner, it is as much scalpel as it is sword. Each shares a sharp blade and each has the same purpose: to destroy that which is bad and which must be removed. Saint Paul uses the same imagery to get at the same truth. This war requires well-trained soldiers, warriors skilled at the sword. This is as true as the day is long. The enemy has a massive arsenal, a stockpile of weapons and munitions in the form of temptations, doubts, excitement of the passions, pride set against God's commands.

This is why Simeon speaks as he does to Mary. The Son of God, His Firstborn, has been presented to the Father according to the command of the Father. His inheritance from the Father will be an everlasting kingdom, as His angel told Mary at the Annunciation almost a year earlier. But that kingdom would be established in bloody warfare, for the enemy was in this fight to the death.

"Behold, this child is set for the fall and rising of many in Israel" (Luke ii:34). Simeon is careful to speak in the correct order when he says "fall and rising" as opposed to "rising and fall." When historians look backward and catalogue the movement of empires and kingdoms, they always speak from the perspective of the future, gazing backward in time. But Simeon, enlightened by the Holy Spirit, witnessed history before it happened. He beheld the destruction of the current kingdom first and only then the establishment of the everlasting kingdom.

He saw this as he contemplated the Babe. He knew in advance that the current kingdom, the current status quo, would not go quietly. It would rage against Him, this tiny Child, so much so that He would Himself be a walking sign of contradiction between the two armies. He would be more than leader of one side; He would offer Himself on the contradicting beams of the Cross, with one beam pointing to Heaven and the other swiping the earth horizontally.

And none of this could happen without the sword. Open battle would have to be engaged in the very near future. His army would be His Church—His Church Militant created to fight, where every member was "born for combat." The price of victory would be being gutted. The prize of victory would be Himself. The weapon of war would be the sword, which appears here fittingly as the first rays of dawn of the day of battle.

It would be many years in the future, but Our Blessed Lord would direct the thoughts of His Holy Mother back to this encounter with Simeon, where the old man prophesies that She would bear in the suffering of Her Son as He fulfills obediently the assignment of His Heavenly Father. So here at the very beginning is the sword, and

23

the warning of the sword from an inside source, Simeon. His holiness allowed him to peer into the future and understand the eternally high stakes being fought. No one would ever be able to set foot in the soon-to-be Kingdom without dripping and soaking in blood.

That the victim soul who would have to suffer the most would be His own Mother, the Immaculate, is the warning we have of the magnitude of sin, the depths of its ugliness. If we glance at the crucifix, we must not do so without realizing the reality of sin. It is so repugnant, so antithetical to God, that this suffering Servant had to undergo this torture as a small way to help us understand how horrible is the reality of sin. So too is the suffering for those who participate in His work. The closer one is to the Divine, the more one must participate in the Sacrifice, the Cross. The one who is closest has the deepest sharing in the suffering. The one closest is His Mother, the Woman of Genesis, the Queen.

Reserved for Her would be the pains of childbirth, which She did not undergo as She brought forth Grace in the stable. She was to be Mother of Him, not just in His body, but also of His Mystical Body. The pains She had not experienced in Bethlehem She would undergo on Golgotha. She was to be Mother of the Church, of all believers, and this birth would not be without pains.

No one escapes the sword—not the King, not the Queen, not the Kingdom. When God was pronouncing judgment on King David for his murder and adultery, He declared to him that the sword would never depart your house. And now, the daughter of David would feel the effects of that sword the most keenly.

Simeon knew. He had been told, it had been revealed to him by Heaven, that the sword would be drawn against and thrust into the holiest of all humans, that Her soul would be pierced. Such is the price of glory with God—earthly agony in exchange for an everlasting crown. It was to fall to Simeon to be the bearer of the news of the sword.

Chapter 5

THE FIFTH JOYFUL MYSTERY:

The Finding of the Child Jesus in the Temple

Aside from a few details, including the flight into Egypt and Our Lord's life in Nazareth, the Holy Spirit has kept hidden from us on the parchment of Scripture much of the life of Our Lord. There is much historical fact shielded from our knowledge. But there is this singular exception with the account of Our Lord as a twelve-year-old Child being found by Our Lady and St. Joseph in the Temple after having been deprived of His physical presence for three days.

There is much to contemplate in this scene. For example, there is the reality that in twenty more years the leaders of the Temple would successfully plot to kill this young Man. They would conspire against Him, as He would in future speak of destroying the Temple and rebuilding it. He would return here in twenty years to turn over tables of the avaricious moneychangers and whip them out of the Temple precincts. He would stand in the Temple and unleash a sevenfold indictment against the religious leaders for their many sins.

But for now, He sat among them, the teachers and the doctors of the law, launching His first subtle strikes. "After three days they found him in the temple, sitting among the teachers, listening to them and asking them questions" (Luke ii:46). This is the first instance in Sacred Scripture where we hear of Our Lord speaking, and while the Holy Spirit has seen fit to keep from our minds the precise content of the Son's questions, He has revealed to us that the content and depth of the questions were so jarring that those hearing Him were astonished.

Let the historical record therefore reveal that from the first account of Our Blessed Lord's encounter with the enemy, it is He who goes on the attack, the offensive, fully brandishing the sword from Heaven. And yes, it is the enemy He is attacking in the form of his handiwork in the minds of the religious leaders.

Their work, the day-to-day of their lives, was the contemplation of God, His statutes, His laws, His decrees. This was the diet of their intellectual appetites, that by which they were distinguished from the rest of the Chosen People. And now, sitting in encampment about their God made visible, they were thunderstruck by His questions aimed at their intellects.

There is a lesson here for the Catholic in love with souls. Ask questions of the unbelievers, of the poorly formed. Force them to analyze their holdings, thoughts, opinions, philosophies. This realm of the unbelievers cannot bear up against the attacks of Catholic truth. There are various forms of confrontation; ques-tioning is one of them.

We can only leave to the realms of speculation and private revelation the specific content of Our Lord's questions, but much is revealed in the reaction of the teachers and the doctors of the law. Some of them must have been far from God, despite their privileged public status as interpreters of Him and His ways. He must have revealed to them in His questioning the truth of how far their hearts were from Him. Certainly they were astonished at His knowledge divulged in question form, but He had not come to them to enlighten their minds about the secrets of the material world but of the spiritual realm.

He was, after all, about His Father's business. "Did you not know that I must be in my Father's house?" (Luke ii:49). And His Father's business is always directed toward the revelation of truth, so that those created in His image and likeness would come to Him. Too, these were the fathers and older relatives of the ones who would cry out "Crucify Him!" and "We have no king but Caesar." It is, in fact, worth considering that some of those men may very well have been sitting at this event. It would only be, after all, another eighteen years before He would emerge from the secrecy of His hidden life in Nazareth and begin the official proclamation of His Good News.

This was an early shot across Satan's bow, a revelation of how much He wished to engage the enemy, to set twisted minds straight, to have the truths of Heaven contemplated correctly. And to further underscore His desire for this, He sat there in the Temple for three straight days, unbudging, until the call of His Immaculate Mother summoned Him to return with them to Nazareth. He responded to Her voice in His ears by ceasing the current engagement. A few years later, the sound of Her voice in His ears again would this time launch Him on His mission of the "Father's business" to its completion. For now, it was enough to return in humble submission to the town noted for being unable to produce anything good.

There are some parallels to be drawn here from the public life of Our Lord. This was the first public act of His recorded in the Scriptures. His last public act would be to pray for forgiveness for the sons of these men, and quite possibly for some of the very men who would hail Caesar but crucify their King.

Returning to the point of conflict, the first scene of Our Lord's life was in the Temple—altogether fitting, since the Temple was constructed for Him. He came to His own first. He came to His own in the earthly dwelling they had constructed for Him. Thirteen years earlier, Heaven had sent Gabriel as an emissary to Zechariah in the Temple to announce the coming of John. So it is fitting that the Temple, having the role of the center of Jewish life, of the Chosen People, would be the place chosen by God to confront evil, to challenge it by a question—a question so devastating as it was spoken by the Word that the combined intellect of centuries of knowledge of the religious leaders could not answer it and could only sit stunned and marvel.

Christ came to the religious leaders to accuse them of neglect, of not caring for the sheep entrusted to them, of letting the vineyard decay and fall into disrepair. This would not be the last question He

27

would ask them. Years later, in another confrontation, He would answer their question about His authority by posing another question, also in the Temple: From where did John the Baptist receive his commission—from Heaven or from man? Again, they would be left speechless, only this time their thoughts would not be overcome with marvel but with malice, for they began plotting His death.

The "fall" of many that Simeon had foretold to Mary at the time of the Presentation had begun. The pillars of the Temple were beginning to shake, the fall of those who stood in the way was in the offing. Millennia earlier, the fall of mankind had begun as a question from the serpent to Eve: Did God really say you can eat nothing in the Garden? It was divine retribution that the fall of the serpent's kingdom would, in turn, be heralded by a question.

Chapter 6

THE FIRST LUMINOUS MYSTERY:

The Baptism of Our Lord by John the Baptist

When holy men and women encounter holiness for the first time, they are often thrown into conflict of some sort: Our Blessed Mother at the words of Gabriel; St. Peter before Our Lord: "Depart from me, for I am a sinful man, O Lord" (Luke v:8); Elizabeth with Our Lady: "And why is this granted me, that the mother of my Lord should come to me?" (Luke i:43); and so on.

Holiness is imbued with humility, and that humility renders the holy person confused as to why he would be worthy of a visit from Heaven. Such was also the case with John the Baptist. Through his holiness, he immediately recognized his unworthiness. "I need to be baptized by you, and do you come to me?" (Matt. iii:14).

The sword always demands a response, no matter to whom it is presented. The holy bow before it, the wicked draw their own sword or retreat. Such was the reaction of Judas' band of Roman soldiers and Temple guards when Our Lord told them He was the One for Whom they were looking. The reaction to the truth is always the same but originates from entirely different spheres. A conflict arises in the mind—one from holiness, the other from evil. But holiness quickly develops into docility and obedience, while wickedness develops into fear and loathing and confusion.

On that day when Our Blessed Lord approached His spotless cousin John standing in the Jordan, conflict was brewing, contradiction was in the air. Consider that a crowd was standing nearby witnessing the events. We know this because John made an announcement to them that answered a nearly 2,000-year-old question. Additionally, the voice of the Father was heard from Heaven, causing confusion among the people. The scene itself is replete with challenges—from the obvious question why the Son of God would need baptizing, to the language used by John, to the Holy Spirit driving Our Lord into the desert, to the combat Our Lord undertook with demons and wild beasts.

It must be stated clearly that Our Blessed Lord did not stand in need of baptism. John recognizes this instantly, such that he immediately steps aside and announces that he is the one who should be baptized. The purpose of Our Lord's baptism was to give public witness to His anointing. All the kings of Israel were anointed, all the kings of the Jews. The baptism of Our Lord stands as both a beginning and a foreshadowing of the end of His public ministry. With His baptism He is anointed King of the Jews for the Jews. On the Cross, Pilate would make it official for the Gentiles: Jesus of Nazareth, King of the Jews. What was once only a Jewish reality would become known to the whole race.

Recall that at Our Lord's two trials before Pilate, it was the Jewish leaders who brought forth the question of Our Lord's supremacy as something on which to convict Him. The first time was a theological charge. "[H]e has made himself the Son of God" (John xix:7). Pilate had no interest in their theology and passed. Then after a visit to Herod, who returned Him to Pilate, the Jewish leaders acknowledged the reality of Who Jesus was without directly realizing it. "If you release this man, you are not Caesar's friend; every one who makes himself a king sets himself against Caesar. . . . We have no king but Caesar" (John xix:12, 15). This was the charge that got Pilate's attention. A rival King, a threat to the established order—this could not be passed over.

The public Kingship of Christ goes back to the waters of the River Jordan by John's action in baptizing Him. From this moment onward, Our Lord would speak continually about the Kingdom, the need for repentance, and the cross required to enter it. But every public assignment of kingship needs a witness and authority to grant it. John had no authority to make Christ king. But he did have the grace to confer a baptism of anointing because Our Lord granted it to Him. Years before, while in the womb, John had leapt for joy at the arrival of the King, carried in on the throne of Mary. He had been overcome in his mother's water in the womb, which for him became the font of baptism. John had been baptized in water by Our Lord. Today, he would reverse that and anoint Him with water Who had baptized him.

Water itself is a contradiction. It has the power to give life and the power to destroy. The waters of baptism are symbolic of both aspects: death and life in Christ Jesus, dying to ourselves, arising to Christ. We drown and die to our sins but then are restored to life, literally cleansed by the same waters. The aim of the water is not to kill us, but to kill the sin and prepare us for radiance. So important is this first step that Our Blessed Lord said without it there can be no salvation.

John had the authority to perform the baptism, but the effect of the baptism was testified to by the Supreme Witness: the Father. "Thou art my beloved Son; with thee I am well pleased" (Luke iii:22). This was heard by lesser witnesses. It was testified to by John, repeated by the evangelist, stamped with the seal of the Father in His declaration that He had made a thousand years earlier through the second psalm of David. "You are my son, today I have begotten you" (Ps. ii:7).

From all eternity God knew He would take on flesh and assault the rebellious kingdom of the fallen angels. He knew too that nations and kingdoms would be deceived by the deceiver. So here at the scene of the anointing of the King Who would challenge the usurper, the words of the second psalm are echoed at the River Jordan. But there is more here than just a testimony to the identity of Our Blessed Lord; there is the announcement of the mission. The words of the psalm announce much more than just the Sonship of Christ. Consider the context:

> "I have set my king
>   on Zion, my holy hill."
> I will tell of the decree of the Lord:
> He said to me, "You are my son,

today I have begotten you.
Ask of me, and I will make the nations your heritage,
    and the ends of the earth your possession.
You shall break them with a rod of iron,
    and dash them in pieces like a potter's vessel."
Now therefore, O kings, be wise;
    be warned, O rulers of the earth.
Serve the Lord with fear,
    with trembling kiss his feet,
lest he be angry, and you perish in the way;
    for his wrath is quickly kindled.
Blessed are all who take refuge in him. (Ps. ii:6–11)

Yes, He is Son, but He is also King, and He is being set up here as the One Who will smash all pretenders to the throne of the Most High. The baptism of Our Lord is the open declaration of war against Satan that Heaven has now commenced.

Recall that after the upcoming forty days in the desert, Satan will consider the possibility that before him, hungry and tired, veiled in flesh, is the Son. He still does not know it, but something is different with this One from all the previous men of God he has encountered. He knows the psalm. He knows the announcement that the Son will also be the King to rule with an iron rod. What he does not yet know is that this One is the One. Thus the phrasing of eventual temptations, following forty days of fasting and doing battle with demons, none of which could get Him to give in. "If you are the Son of God . . ." (Matt. iv:6). In fact, so rock steady was He and so unable were they to move Him to sin that their lord and master Satan himself had to come to the desert to investigate for himself.

Notice again the question, implicit as it may have been. Satan never commands; he can't. He places questions, raises doubts, makes suggestions. But now, for once, the shoe was on the other hoof. It was Christ Who was placing the doubts, raising the question, causing the uncertainty, offering the "temptation" of wonder to the tempter par excellence. Christ is always in control, and He continued to control the situation from first to last.

Notice also that Satan, no doubt recalling the words of the Holy Spirit in that same second psalm—that all the nations would be subject to the King, the Son—takes Jesus to a high overlook and offers the kingdoms of the earth in exchange for homage, for worship reserved to God alone. The question has been raised whether all of that was ever Satan's to offer to begin with; nonetheless, he used the ploy. The warp and woof of the second psalm must have been and still is a cause of pain for Satan. It is the descriptor of his final defeat, the reality that whatever he possesses, it is not his, and it will be taken back from him by the Son.

But here on the banks of the Jordan, all this was being foreshadowed. How it would be won back was not entirely clear, until a strange apparition presented itself—the Holy Spirit descending on Christ in the form of a dove. This presentation of the Holy Spirit as a dove occurs nowhere else in all of Sacred Scripture; and that is because there is no other moment like this in Sacred Scripture.

Only once is Our Lord anointed for His Kingship and His Sonship. His body will be anointed two more times—in preparation for His burial and at His burial—but those anointings are of a different kind from this one. They will signify the drawing to an end of His work and its completion. This anointing is to announce the beginning of His work and its everlasting effects.

Here, the Holy Spirit descends on Him as a precursor to His Sacrifice. The dove was the sacrificial offering of the poor in the days of the Temple, so the First Person of the Trinity announces the beginning of the fulfillment of the prophecy of David, and the Third Person seals that announcement by revealing how it will be fulfilled: through sacrifice, through the sword.

This is the second time the Holy Trinity has manifested itself directly in the gospels—the first being the Annunciation, where Our Lord was incarnated in the waters of His Immaculate Mother's womb, and now in the waters of baptism, made pure by His anointing. John, standing by, witnesses all of this and to the attendant crowd proclaims the answer to the question asked by Isaac nearly 2,000 years earlier at the scene of his near-sacrifice by his father Abraham. "Behold, the fire and the wood; but where is the lamb for a burnt offering?" (Gen. xxii:7). Abraham responded that God Himself would provide the sacrifice.

John, overcome with the joy the awareness of God's plan unfolding right before his eyes brings about, shouts to the crowd, "Behold, the Lamb of God, who takes away the sin of the world!" (John i:29). It is more than likely there were many people traveling to Jerusalem with their sacrificial lambs in tow. Imagine the scene when they were pointed to a Man standing in the water, with a sacrificial dove fluttering over Him, a voice from Heaven declaring the second Psalm, and the baptizer calling him a lamb.

The contradiction, the challenge to the Jewish mind of the day, must have been remarkable. The second psalm spoke of a son, a king, who would rule the nations with an iron rod. The dove, the lamb, spoke of sacrifice for sin. How could these be reconciled? It was a question that the diabolical was wondering about and asking itself as well. Hell would ask in person, once the coolness of the waters of the Jordan had given way to the heat and dryness of the desert. But Hell would not receive the answer it wanted to know, not yet, anyway.

Chapter 7

THE SECOND LUMINOUS MYSTERY:

The Self-Manifestation of the Lord at the Wedding Feast at Cana

The first public miracle performed by the Son of God took place at a wedding feast. How entirely fitting that God, Who had been present "in the beginning" at the first wedding, would now arrive to confer His blessing on this wedding at the start of His mission.

Frequently in the life of Our Lord, various actions or words take on the role of pointing to the larger while never diminishing the present. The wedding at Cana is one such time. Without lessening the importance of this gathering in the least, it points to the larger reality that His mission would bring about the everlasting nuptials of Him and His Heavenly Bride, the Catholic Church, the smaller always pointing to the larger while retaining its present significance.

It must have been quite the wedding. Our Lord was there. His Holy Mother was there—and not just present but attentive, as She always is. There was so much merriment and so many people that the wine was exhausted early. This would have been a great embarrassment for the bride and groom and for their families, a much greater embarrassment than contemporary man might imagine.

Hospitality was a deeply valued attribute in the Middle East. The extreme living conditions made hospitality a virtual requirement in order to preserve life. The climate was harsh, the geography rough, and escape from the heat hard to attain. So hospitality to the stranger was a near commandment. Given that the stranger needed to be treated with such hospitality, how much more generously would friends and relatives need to be treated, expect to be treated? To run out of wine at your own wedding would have been the height of insult to the assembled guests.

So Our Blessed Mother, mindful of the shame that would be forth-coming, turns to Her Divine Son, Whom She knows can immediately solve the issue, and informs Him—with the implication that She desires that He solve it. And here, the sword is drawn again, only this time, it is more than a warning; it is the promise that if he does this for Her, Her pain will begin.

He says three things to Her, all of which have the effect of drawing the sword closer. He first says, "Woman," immediately raising the context from the earthly to the spiritual. By calling Her Woman, He is invoking Her royal title, pointing to Her as the Wo-man of prophecy, the Woman of Genesis. He does not call Her "Mother," for that is too immediate to the relationship between Him and Her.

This action will expand Her role from just His Mother to Queen and Mother of all. This will come with a price, a heavy cost to Her. He then reminds Her of the closeness between the two of them, that what affects Him affects Her as well. The idiom He employs is best translated as "What to Thee, to Me" (John ii:4). Whatever happens to me happens to you, and whatever happens to you happens to me. So closely are We united, Mother, joined together since Your "fiat," that if I set foot on My mission, then You set foot on that mission with Me.

Recall, Mother, what Simeon said to You all those years ago: that a sword would pierce Your own soul, Your own heart. That My pain, My suffering, would be felt by You in Your own being. This is why He adds the seeming non sequitur in various translations, "My hour has not yet come" (John ii:4). He is laying it at the feet of His Blessed Mother to launch Him on His Pilgrimage of Grace, on His crusade against the serpent. The Woman of Genesis Who brought Him to the world would now be the One to command that the first shot be fired.

As is always the case, notice who is the aggressor in the war for the souls of men. God is never on the defensive; He is never scrambling. He is always the proactive One, the attacker. He sits back and waits for the opportune moment—and then He unleashes. It was altogether fitting that since a woman's actions had begun the cascade of events that led to the fall of man, that God in His magnanimity would give a Woman the opportunity to begin the cascade of events that would bring about ~~his~~ man's redemption.

He handed Her the sword and asked Her to consider that, if She signaled war, She would plunge the sword into Her own immaculate soul. She would no longer be just the earthly Mother of Jesus, but She would now become the Mother of all believers, the Mediatrix of all grace, the Queen of Heaven. What She had brought about at its beginning in private She would now complete in public.

So Our Blessed Lord, Her little Boy, Whose knees She had bandaged, Whose head She had kissed, Whose little body She had rocked to sleep, now left it to Her to decide the moment of battle. Without hesitation or consideration of Her own suffering, She turned to the head waiter and instructed, "Do whatever he tells you" (John ii:5), the last recorded words of Holy Mary in Sacred Scripture.

In one of the most contrasted moments in all Holy Writ, it was not God Who launched the first volley, but His own Mother. She knew where the road ahead ended. She knew there would be intensity of suffering. She had known, in some degree of mystery, that Her pains would be incalculable—for the purer a creature is, the greater the pain when witnessing sin. And there would be for Her no greater pain than to witness Her own Son undergoing what He endured as She stood there at the Cross three years hence.

Yet knowing all that, She gave the order: Attack! Reveal yourself. Begin the war to beat back the serpent. Free the race. Set out on Your mission. Save My children whom I will hold in My immaculate womb on Golgotha. *Attack!*

The first miracle of Our Lord contained within itself a contradiction —after all, He was a sign of contradiction, as Simeon had prophesied. He created new wine out of old. The former water now become wine was incredibly good, so much so that the captain of the feast accused the party of saving the "best for last." But how could this be?

Good wine is always aged; it is always old. But this wine had just sprung into existence moments earlier. God had just created fresh and new from something old. It was a foretaste of the many paradoxes that would accompany Him, His words, and His actions. And the miracle for proof that Satan had tried to trick out of Him He freely gave to the Woman Who would crush his head.

The first miracle points to the fact that without pain, there is no salvation, no redemption—there is only enslavement. Salvation contains within it a degree of mystery the mind cannot explain, should not attempt to explain. What is desired by God is an affirmation to the questions: "Do you wish Me to begin my work of salvation within you?" "Are you willing to partake in My suffering for your salvation and the salvation of others?"

He would later ask His disciples a related question: "Are you able to drink the cup that I am to drink?" (Matt. xx:22). The wine in that chalice would not be the "best" saved until the "last." That wine would be the dregs that would bring about salvation. So horrifying is the thought of drinking that wine that Our Blessed Lord asked three times in His agony that, if it be possible, this wine pass Him by. He had created the best of the wine for the wedding guests at the request of His Mother. He Himself would consume the most pungent, horrid wine that existed at the request of His Father. The first was done for revelers at the wedding. The second was done for captives. Anyone who follows Christ must join in the combat of drinking bitter wine, of consuming the chalice laid before us.

Here too we have one of those themes in the life of Our Lord, one of those many instances when an event that is real and significant in its own right points to a greater significance, matches up to a far larger reality. Our Blessed Lord's mission begins with a cup of wine and reaches its climax with a chalice of wine in the Garden. It begins at a wedding where He has set foot on the path that will lead to a wedding without end—where He will forever wed Himself to His Bride by dying for Her.

Chapter 8

THE THIRD LUMINOUS MYSTERY:

The Proclamation of the Kingdom and the Call to Conversion

Each of the mysteries has contained within itself a point of conflict or combat. Each meditation presents us with a challenge, both from the moment in history and in the current spiritual life of each of us. This is why the Rosary is so effective as a weapon. It is a weapon. It is a sword, a powerful weapon in the spiritual arsenal because of the discipline required to pray it, and the concentration required to contemplate each mystery.

What is a mystery, other than something you continue to plumb to find, to discover, increasing meaning, without ever reaching the conclusion? If a mystery's secrets were exhausted, it would no longer be a mystery. One of the secrets in each of these mysteries is the aspect of combat, of fight, of sheer willpower and determination needed to overcome the obstacle. The Catholic life is all about fighting, overcoming the challenges, combating the darkness in us and around us.

This requires a docility and willingness to learn about our weaknesses and the consequent need to face them down and defeat them. The first among those internal enemies is pride—the egotistical character within us that never accepts blame or responsibility for wrongdoing. To this specific point, Our Blessed Lord aimed His first artillery shot. The first words He spoke in His public mission were "Repent, for the kingdom of heaven is at hand" (Matt. iv:17). Our Lord picks up right where John the Baptist leaves off. The mission is twofold: to preach the Kingdom and to die for its subjects.

The work of His Mystical Body will be to round up as many as will hear the preaching into the Kingdom before the end of the world.

There is an urgency about the preaching, an insistence that now is the time, that time is short. There is in the midst of all this the declaration that Heaven and Hell are at war, that there are two kingdoms. His will be the victorious one and the other the vanquished. But there is also the warning, the grim news that what is required of His army is complete and total sacrifice.

It will be news that will not be heard and accepted by most. At the heart of the news of the Kingdom is the startling revelation that He Himself is Heaven. He is the "image of the invisible God" (Col. i:15), that He is the great "I Am." His hearers, for the most part, could not believe what they were hearing; it was too offensive to religious sensibilities.

He was asked: "Are you saying you are greater than Moses?" "Are you greater than our father Abraham, who died?" (John viii:53). Not only was He saying He was, but that He was in fact much more. It was not until the moment of the trial before the Sanhedrin that He gave the clear public affirmation they had guessed right about what He was saying.

Caiaphas asked Him, "Are you the Christ, the Son of the Blessed?" (Mark xiv:61). It was here, at the end of the mission, that He would give answer to that which He had earlier refused to Satan in the desert. He would not answer him, but He would answer the offspring of Satan, those to whom He had earlier said that their father was the devil because they did their father's will. The only father he would answer would be His own. But the children, He was sent to them; and when they asked point blank, He gave a point-blank response. "I am; and you will see the Son of man sitting at the right hand of Power, and coming with the clouds of heaven" (Mark xiv:62). That was what they needed to hear, and so began the final phase of bringing about His death.

They would object vociferously when Pilate wrote the inscription "King of the Jews" above His crowned head on the Cross. They had no king but Caesar, they had earlier cried out. This was an insult, offensive to their sensibilities. Those who object to Truth will always be offended.

The spiritual combat occurring in this mystery of the Rosary is a combat of faith. Our Blessed Lord had to convey certain truths to His audience in such a manner that they could grasp a deeper meaning. Without faith, this would not be possible. Frequently, He would draw out the faith of a person before performing a miracle. Oftentimes, He would conclude by offering that their faith in Him had saved them.

But what was it He was asking of them—faith in what, precisely? At one point He proclaimed that the Kingdom of Heaven was at hand—and it was. But on another occasion He made it quite clear that "at hand" meant something different from just a reference to an event close in time to arriving.

The Kingdom had already arrived, was there for them to look at immediately. "[T]he kingdom of God is in the midst of you" (Luke xvii:21). What is Heaven, after all? It is where God dwells. But even more profoundly, since God dwells within Himself, He is the Kingdom, and it is therefore "among you." How truly He spoke when He replied to Pilate, "My kingship is not of this world" (John xviii:36); it is otherworldly.

Pilate looked straight at Heaven, straight at Truth, and completely missed it. In the greatest case in human history of missing what's right under your nose, Pilate is the man. Pilate would have none of this threat to his worldly kingdom. After further attempted negotiation with the bloodthirsty Jewish leaders, he gave in, and delivered Heaven into the hands of Hell.

It could be said there was one long descent into Hell by Our Lord. But it would not be said that Hell would win. Heaven is so powerful, so majestic, that it willingly accepts Hell's greatest thrust, its most powerful, most dreaded weapon—death—and turns it around. The crown of thorns would become the royal crown, the spear the scepter, the Cross the throne. All would be accomplished by the Kingdom. The kingdom of death, ruled by the rebellious legions, would be defeated by the kingdom of life, a personal kingdom—so personal it was all balled up into the Person of Christ. How powerful is God, how supreme is Jesus Christ, that He single-handedly defeated an entire kingdom, for the point that Satan, like Pilate, completely missed was that this God-Man was the Kingdom of Heaven.

Heaven is not a place so much as it is a Person, or rather Three Persons. This one God vanquished an entire kingdom in one act. What absurdity, what folly, to consider now that Satan in the desert offered to the Kingdom of Heaven the kingdoms of the world in exchange for homage. In retrospect (for Satan has a memory), his humiliation must be increased all the more when he considers the profound idiocy of his temptation.

For His earthly preaching, Our Blessed Lord spent years—three of them—trying to help feebleminded men come to the reality of what the Kingdom was, what it was worth, and how it was achieved. The short answer was: It is Christ Himself, and it is worth everything you could pay. He drew this out time and again.

> The kingdom of heaven is like treasure hidden in a field, which a man found and covered up; then in his joy he goes and sells all that he has and buys that field. Again, the kingdom of heaven is like a merchant in search of fine pearls, who, on finding one pearl of great value, went and sold all that he had and bought it. Again, the kingdom of heaven is like a net which was thrown into the sea and gathered fish of every kind; when it was full, men drew it ashore and sat down and sorted the good into vessels but threw away the bad. So it will be at the close of the age. The angels will come out and separate the evil from the righteous, and throw them into the furnace of fire; there men will weep and gnash their teeth. (Matt. xiii:44–50)

Three times in this passage we hear the word "like" in relation to Heaven. But all three instances speak of Heaven in the present tense, not some futuristic sense alone. If you substitute "Jesus" for

"Heaven," then it becomes much clearer. Yes, there is of course the futuristic, everlasting sense, without a doubt; but there is also the present sense of Heaven.

Notice that both the man who finds the treasure in the field and the merchant in search of fine pearls are both presently active and working and achieving something in the present. They have their reward now; they are in current possession of it. This does not preclude an ever greater experience of it in the future, but it must be accepted that the current situation is the cause of much excitement for them.

The man who finds the treasure wants it in the here and now for his own. He covers it up so as not to lose control of it to another passerby and quickly runs off to sell every possession he has. He recognizes right now the value right now—the Heaven on earth, not just in the afterlife. And it causes him much joy. He was not even looking for it, yet he knows a good thing when he discovers it.

This is how it is for the man who discovers Christ when not even looking for Him. He "trips" across Him, so to speak. Imagine the awe of the man in the field when he opened the chest buried just beneath the surface. His search was over. He may not have even had conscious knowledge of being on a search for anything. But he had a moment when it all became stunningly clear to him—and with that, in the twinkling of an eye, everything changed.

It must have been like that in the Upper Room on that first Easter Sunday night when Our Lord suddenly appeared to the Apostles. Instantly, they were present to Heaven; or rather, the Kingdom had come to them, was made present to them. The moment of the finding of Heaven is life-shattering. Nothing else matters except the Kingdom, because the Kingdom is a Person. Truly, His Kingdom is not of this world. No earthly king has ever been able to claim himself as the kingdom, only the king. The monarch may die, the king may die—long live the king—but the kingdom outlives the king. That is true of kingdoms of this world. It is not true of the Kingdom of Heaven.

The man sells everything! Consider that outlandish statement. He sells everything he owns. He gives no consideration to anything other than owning the treasure. That purity of heart, that single object of desire, would be spoken of again by Our Blessed Lord when He said of Himself, "[L]ay up for yourselves treasures in heaven, where neither moth nor rust consumes and where thieves do not break in and steal" (Matt. vi:20).

But there is the exchange required. All prior longings, lusts, desires, riches—all of them must be abandoned. Nothing of the past can be held onto—not family, not friendships, not careers—nothing that will block the newfound love. All other loves must go.

There is an interesting and revealing use of words between Matthew's Gospel and Luke's, specifically Matthew 10:37 and Luke 9:61–62.

Luke recounts: "Another said, 'I will follow you, Lord; but let me first say farewell to those at my home.' Jesus said to him, 'No one who puts his hand to the plow and looks back is fit for the kingdom of God'" (Luke ix:61–62).

Matthew recounts: "He who loves father or mother more than me is not worthy of me; and he who loves son or daughter more than me is not worthy of me" (Matt. x:37).

Notice the equality He makes between Heaven and Himself. The same person wanting to spend time with family is not worthy of both the Kingdom of God and Himself. They are excluded from each, because they are each the same. Jesus is Heaven because wherever Jesus is, so too is Father and Spirit. So when Our Lord preaches as His opening salvo to the world, "Repent, for the kingdom of Heaven is at hand," He is preaching in reality that now is the moment, repent, because I am here.

In two different circumstances, Our Blessed Lord uses the expression "at hand." In either case, given the context, is He meaning something upcoming, in the near future? He means now. This may not be as evident in the first circumstance, such as above, when He says the Kingdom of Heaven is at hand, but it is abundantly clear in the more immediate sense when He says to the Apostles in Gethsemane, "'[S]ee, my betrayer is at hand.' While he was still speaking, Judas came, one of the twelve, and with him a great crowd with swords and clubs, from the chief priests and the elders of the people" (Matt. xxvi:46–47).

When Our Blessed Lord employs the phrase "at hand," He means "this moment." So when He speaks of the Kingdom being at hand, He means this moment, now, because His divine presence, redemption, and salvation have come to you right now. It is not a matter of waiting for the train to arrive or the ship to dock; they have already done so. It means: Climb on board now, for the moment is here. Repent now.

But what repentance entails is not something every man or woman is willing to pay. Not everyone wants to climb aboard or is willing to pay the fare. In fact, most will not. The path is not easy, and the way is difficult. Our Lord calls Himself "the way." The way to Heaven is Heaven. The glory of this truth was grasped by St. Catherine of Siena. "All the way to heaven is heaven, because Jesus said, 'I am the way.' So Jesus is heaven, and He is the way to Heaven."

But following the way to Heaven is riddled with pain and suffering. The way requires pain because the way Himself endured pain, bore the Cross. There is no other way, for there is no other name under Heaven by which men are saved. Heaven is the Kingdom. The Kingdom is the way. The way is Our Lord. Our Lord is Heaven. He is the treasure, the pearl of great price. He does not give these things; He is these things—these things and much more.

In a final presentation of this to His intimates, the Apostles, He relates at the Last Supper in a most astounding way that He Himself is the new and everlasting covenant. When He took the cup, He said, "This is my blood of the covenant, which is poured out for many" (Mark xiv:24). There is a sameness He establishes between His Blood and the covenant. They are the same, which is why the covenant, this covenant, is everlasting, because it is He Himself. He is the covenant. It is He Who cannot ever be broken, abolished, or done away with. The blood is not a symbol of the covenant. That was what the rainbow to Noah was. A symbol points to a reality. It is the reality to which we cling.

Christ Jesus Himself is the new and everlasting covenant promised to His followers, so when we say we are redeemed in His Blood, indeed we are. We are saved by the Blood of the Passion, absolutely. A symbol has no intrinsic power. If it did, it would move from symbol to reality. The Blood is not a symbol of the covenant—it *is* the covenant. A symbol does not have the power to save. Only the reality has that. And the Blood of Christ, the Real Presence, is Jesus Christ. So when Christ is held aloft, Heaven has come to earth. "[T]he kingdom of God is in the midst of you" (Luke xvii:21).

Chapter 9

THE FOURTH LUMINOUS MYSTERY:

The Transfiguration

If a soul is searching for combat, for conflict in a particular mystery, the Transfiguration is a good place to begin. It is replete with contradiction, challenge, and conflict. The scene ends in one of confusion and questioning for Peter, James, and John. Days before His Sacred Passion was to begin, Our Blessed Lord prepares the disciples by revealing His glory to them, by dropping the veil of His humanity, so to speak, and allowing them a brief moment to gaze on His divinity.

They had up to this point only begun to guess and conjecture among themselves as to the reality of Who He was. Peter had announced it in Caesarea Philippi when He declared Him the Son of the Living God, after a revelation from the Father. Not only do they see the glory of the only begotten Son, they also behold Moses and Elijah. The representatives of the Law and the Prophets present yet another scene of combat; they are speaking with Him about His forthcoming Passion, His Exodus.

Freeze that thought for a moment. Here stands the Second Person of the Blessed Trinity, resplendent in glory, as two of His forerunners speak with Him of His impending suffering—God in His glory conversing about His agony. Now there is a meditation point on the continual conflict, the tension the Catholic must face each day.

Peter has entirely missed the point of what is happening. He is listening at one moment to the discussion going on among Our Lord, Moses, and Elijah, where they are speaking about what is to happen, and yet, completely disregarding this, Peter puts forth that they should all plant themselves here on the mountain by erecting three tabernacles, or tents.

So off the mark is his observation it is not even recognized, acknowledged, or responded to by Our Lord, to Whom it was addressed. They cannot stay on the mountain. The mission is to die in Jerusalem, not maintain a life of ease and piety on the mountain. There is deep conflict here, conflict within the soul of Peter, who now for a second time tries to dissuade Our Lord from His mission. The first time drew a rebuke from Our Lord; this one draws silence.

While Peter is still fumbling about, the next moment brings the cloud that terrifies the three disciples—and with good reason. The cloud always represented the presence of God, present yet not touchable, transcendent while still immanent. For a second time in the life of Our Lord, the voice of the Father is heard—and not just heard, but reiterating what He had said at the banks of the Jordan. "This is my beloved Son, with whom I am well pleased; listen to him" (Matt. xvii:5).

This time, however, instead of just presenting the relationship between them as Father and Son, as He did at Our Lord's baptism, He adds "listen to Him." What did Jesus say that needed listening to?

"If any man would come after me, let him deny himself and take up his cross daily and follow me. For whoever would save his life will lose it; and whoever loses his life for my sake, he will save it. For what does it profit a man if he gains the whole world and loses or forfeits himself?" (Luke ix:23–25).

"Behold, I send you out as sheep in the midst of wolves; so be wise as serpents and innocent as doves. Beware of men; for they will deliver you up to councils, and flog you in their synagogues, and you will be dragged before governors and kings for my sake, to bear testimony before them and the Gentiles" (Matt. x:16–18).

"Brother will deliver up brother to death, and the father his child, and children will rise against parents and have them put to death; and you will be hated by all for my name's sake. But he who endures to the end will be saved" (Matthew x:21–22).

"Do not think that I have come to bring peace upon the earth. I have come to bring not peace but the sword. For I have come to set a man against his father, a daughter against her mother, and a daughter-in-law against her mother-in-law; and one's enemies will be those of his household" (Matt. x:34-35).

"[A]nd he who does not take his cross and follow me is not worthy of me" (Matt. x:38).

These are just a small sampling of what Our Lord warned His disciples about the cost of their following Him. The sword, present at His presentation in the Temple to His Blessed Mother, is now drawn for all His followers. The sword, division, hatred, family strife, persecution, rejection, martyrdom, governments and kings aligned against them—everything that Hell could throw at them would come their way.

In a sense, to whatever degree Peter may have processed all these warnings over the prior three years, it is understandable why he would want to stay on the mountain. But staying was not the course; confronting, doing combat with these forces, is the order of the day, every day. The Cross never leaves the Catholic life just as the sword will never depart the house of David. We are his heirs, and part of the inheritance is the sword, transformed into the Cross by the new King of Israel.

There will be no staying on the mountain—not for the disciples nor for us. There is a war to fight, a combat to wage, souls to save. There is witness to give, blood to be shed, persecutions to undergo, crosses to carry, martyrdoms to be had. And in a frightening conclusion to all these, Our Blessed Lord says, "[H]e who endures to the end will be saved" (Matt. xxiv:13). One of the saints has commented that the only way to win this war is to die fighting it. There is no retreat, no respite. The combat is spiritual, and the spiritual never rests.

If all of this were not jarring enough for the Apostles as they walked down the mountain, they heard the instruction from Our Lord to tell no one about this until He had been raised from the dead. And then there arose the further conflict in their minds what "raised from the dead" meant. While the mystery of the Transfiguration is beautiful to imagine, it is also frightening in its implications for the Catholic and his daily life. The glory of Christ is revealed specifically to show a counterbalance to the evil that must be endured.

The more glorious Our Lord in the vision, the more correspondingly ugly that which must be fought against. The Catholic life is not for the spiritually wimpy. It is not for the weak, the weary, the complainers. It is for none who would eventually drop the cross and not persevere. This is the thought that must permeate the mind when meditating on this mystery: the need for perseverance in the face of struggle. Saint Alphonsus Ligouri stressed how much we must each pray for perseverance, the necessity of being true to our dying breath.

This is the message of this mystery: that the battle must be engaged, there can be no retreat into simplistic piety, and we must come down off the mountain and fight.

Chapter 10

THE FIFTH LUMINOUS MYSTERY:

The Institution of the Holy Eucharist

The specific meditation associated with this mystery can include a number of scenes—the Last Supper, certainly, but also the announcement of the Holy Eucharist at the synagogue in Capernaum the day after the miracle of the loaves. If one is looking for a scene more filled with hostility, it would be difficult to locate one in Scripture. Consider that the unruly Jews the day before had hailed Our Lord as "the prophet" because He had multiplied the loaves and fish in the wilderness.

Their cries related back to Moses' foretelling that a prophet would appear on the scene who would do what he had done with the manna in the desert, so the audience contemporary to Our Lord immediately saw the connection; hence, the cries: "This is indeed the prophet who is to come into the world!" (John vi:14).

The frenzy of the crowd is something Our Lord wanted nothing to do with because it was not inspired by faith in Him, but by food in their bellies. He also ordered His Apostles into the boat and directed them to Capernaum on the far side of the sea, because He did not want them swept up in the adulation of the crowd. And on the other side of the sea, in the synagogue in Capernaum, hometown of Peter, Andrew, James, and John, is where Our Lord chose to unleash His most challenging teaching yet. So much faith did it require that at the end of this episode, that multitude that had hailed Him as prophet not twenty-four hours earlier would now abandon Him. It is the only instance in all the gospels where Our Lord's teaching causes a mass desertion—and with good reason. It is the most faith-demanding. The entire episode begins in hostility and accusations and concludes with apostasy and Judas being called a "devil" (although the specific identity of Judas was kept hidden by Our Lord).

There is a deep lesson for meditation and reflection here as we pray this decade of the Rosary: Our Lord chose this site, time, and place, these people, this crowd to announce that which He knew ahead of time would cause people to reject Him, walk away, and abandon Him. Sometimes, when we are evangelizing or catechizing others, we think in terms of being successful, saying things in the manner that will most likely cause them to convert or revert. Our Blessed Lord knew beforehand that this teaching would mean a wholesale departure of the masses, and yet He preached it anyway.

Nor did He retreat from what He taught and try to win the crowd back. He laid it out there and spoke clear truth. What they did with it, how the masses responded, would be up to the masses. He even turned to His Apostles, who just the day before were so swept up in the excitement of the crowd that Our Lord ordered them to safety. And not only did the crowd not understand this central teaching, but St. Mark tells us that so abysmal was the faith of the Apostles, so uncomprehending of the significance of the miracle of the loaves, that they had difficulty recognizing Our Lord as He approached them on the water when they were rowing for safety. They thought He was a ghost.

A point of meditation here, then, could be always to speak the truth, even when you know what the response will be. It is not that we should seek out conflict, but we must recognize and accept that the teachings of Our Lord are going to be rejected by most people. That rejection, even if we know about it ahead of time, does not absolve us from delivering the truth.

And so to the narrative relayed to us by St. John of that day when Jesus lost His public support and one of His own Twelve turned against Him in his heart. The relevant passage in chapter six of St. John's Gospel begins with the crowd coming to Jesus after having discovered that He and the Apostles had left the south side of the sea and had more than likely rowed to the other side. They traverse around the water and locate Him, as they suspected they would.

Notice, pay close attention to the interchange, right from the beginning. They begin with small talk. "Rabbi, when did you come here?" (John vi:25). But Our Lord knows their hearts, and while dismissing their idle chatter, goes straight for the jugular—and He does so with an oath. "Truly, truly, I say to you, you seek me, not because you saw signs, but because you ate your fill of the loaves" (John vi:26).

He instantly accuses them of unfaithfulness to Him, His miracles, and His mission. Moreover, He charges them with selfishness and egotism. He wants nothing to do with their silly pretense of "dialoguing" about how He arrived on this side of the sea. They feel the sting of His accusation and respond as anyone does when he is discovered—in anger.

He demands that they believe in Him. They demand a sign. Now a curious aside here: As He is giving them the assurance that He is credible and they should have faith in Him, He says that He is the One on Whom the Father has set His seal. The context of the conversation is bread, the loaves. In Our Lord's time, bakers would place their seal on bread, a kind of branding. Seals may have been placed on other things as well, but not on people. That Our Lord says of Himself that He bears a seal from the Father, in the context of a discussion about bread, is significant. He will go on to call Himself the Bread of Life, and He will continue the theme and declare that "the bread which I shall give for the life of the world is my flesh" (John vi:51). The seal hearkens back to the baptism Our Lord received by John the Baptist. The kings of Israel were all sealed, made God's anointed. Our Blessed Lord is pulling out all the stops, as it were, in this confrontation.

Continuing, the skeptical Jews ask what they can do to accomplish the works of God. The answer, in preparation for what they are about to hear from Him, is to believe. In a moment, He is going to reveal to them one of the most sublime mysteries of the universe, and they will have to believe Him. In response to His call for faith, they ask for a sign. Now this is most curious on two fronts. First, He had just performed a sign the day before; that was the reason they followed Him to the other side of the sea. But the charge Our

Lord leveled against them regarding their intentions has hit its mark. They are stung in conscience and so demand a sign from Him to confirm He is "the prophet."

This is why they ask for the sign to be about bread. That is what Moses did in the desert with the manna, and if they are to believe, they say they need to see Him exhibit power like Moses. But Our Lord was greater than Moses, and He dismisses their demands for a sign, and lays aside their near-idolatry of Moses with a rebuke: "Jesus then said to them, 'Truly, truly, I say to you, it was not Moses who gave you the bread from heaven; my Father gives you the true bread from heaven'"(John vi:32).

Again, it is the Father Whose actions are at work here, a point they continually miss. When He declares to them that the bread He has gives life to the world, they have a momentary surge of faith. But their faith is of the natural kind, not the supernatural. They are anticipating that He is going to make magical bread appear that will grant them life, so for this they are willing to keep listening. In fact, they plead, "Lord, give us this bread always" (John vi:34).

For the next few moments, Our Lord enlightens their minds with the profound truth of the Holy Eucharist. He calls Himself Bread —the Bread of Life, the Bread that came down from Heaven, the Bread from the Father, Who, recall, has set His seal on Him, as a Divine Baker. Again, they miss the point, utterly miss the point. They get hung up on the issue of His origin and completely pass over the deeper reality of His mission. He is from God. This they begin discussing among themselves, and they begin doubting what He is saying.

And here, Our Lord, aware of their misgivings, would in human terms have the ability to address their concerns and explain it all to them, to alleviate their worries, massage their misgivings. And most importantly, He does not. In a literary sense, He goes in for the kill. He not only declares He is from Heaven, that the Father has set His divine seal on Him, that He is the Bread of Life, but now He explains exactly what this means. "[T]he bread which I shall give for the life of the world is my flesh" (John vi:51). When the seal of kingship was placed on Him in the waters of the Jordan, John declared Him to be the lamb—the lamb missing from Jewish history for nearly 2,000 years. Yet in the Passover meal, the lamb had to be consumed, eaten, its flesh eaten by those who would be saved.

And so, to their shock and amazement, He thunders that they must eat Him, consume Him, gnaw His Flesh in order to be saved—and what's more, if they didn't, they would die. And in a missive to their request for a miracle comparable to Moses and the manna, He completely turns the tables and says that, as miraculous as the appearance of manna may have been, their ancestors still died in the desert.

He challenges everything they hold dear. He offends every sensibility possible. He tells them to drink His Blood, a complete and total aversion to the Jews. He causes a near-riot to break out among them as they argue with one another over the meaning of His words. Anyone who says that division is not of Christ does not understand what happened this lone morning by the shores of the Sea of Galilee in and around the synagogue of Capernaum. Division is necessary because it makes people profess their belief or lack of belief. There can be no faith without division, for division creates precision, definition, accuracy.

That is what Our Lord demanded in Capernaum on that day—He was precise in what He taught. He left open no other meaning or definition that could be applied. He was deadly accurate, and now He demanded the response. He had issued the ultimate invitation of faith, and now it was up to His followers to accept or reject it. And they rejected it, as does most of the world today, including Protestantism.

Let's return to the opening thought. Our Lord knew this would be the reaction. He knew in advance with absolute certainty that they would no longer walk with Him (John vi:66), and yet He did it anyway. Why? Because the truth cannot be subject to the whims of the mob, driven by their own agendas and motivations. The false motivations must be called out and the truth declared. And here is the take-away, regardless of the outcome—the chips will have to fall where they may, but they must be dropped. No one is above suffering for the truth, not even Truth Himself.

And to reconnect the meditation between Capernaum and the Upper Room at the Last Supper, there was one figure who played a prominent role in both stories, although known at the time only to Our Blessed Lord: Judas. Whatever Judas did on Holy Thursday night, it was born from this experience at Capernaum. He had given his mind over to doubting Jesus, to not believing all this talk about bread and eating flesh. He may have stuck around because he had no place else to go. He may have been too cowardly to reveal his true feelings, like most of the crowd. Whatever his motive or confusion, he stayed, but was a time bomb from this point forward. It is another point worth meditating on and considering that Judas did not go from loyal disciple to traitor in the space of a day or two. How loyal he may or may not have been at the outset is unknown to us.

What we do know is that he betrayed Our Lord on a scale so magnificent that Our Lord cried aloud about it a thousand years earlier in the psalms. "Even my bosom friend in whom I trusted, who ate of my bread, has lifted his heel against me" (Psalm xli:9). Notice Our Lord's cry over bread. The instrument, the sign of the betrayal, would center on bread.

The sign of Judas' betrayal could have centered on various things. He was a thief, a hypocrite regarding care for the poor—any number of things could have signaled his treachery. But it was bread that was highlighted in Our Lord's mourning over his betrayal. Judas' betrayal, even though it was completed in Gethsemane, began in Capernaum—and the cause was his lack of faith in Christ and His announcement of the Eucharist.

Chapter 11

THE FIRST SORROWFUL MYSTERY:

The Agony in the Garden

Another scene of conflict, combat, challenge. Anyone who thinks the Rosary is not a presentation of the fierce combat sometimes required in the spiritual life needs to meditate heavily on this mystery.

We have the struggle Our Lord feels when He sees the suffering before Him and realizes that, despite His efforts, most of humanity will be damned. Even the comparatively trivial struggle for the Apostles to stay awake, and the contradiction between Judas' betrayal and the sign of his treachery—a kiss—all of this is combative. Our Lord even draws the distinction clearly when He approaches the slumbering Apostles and declares that "the spirit indeed is willing, but the flesh is weak" (Matt. xxvi:40). The battle within man never ends until this life ends.

There is the conflict between Our Lord's soul and body, so intense that the body begins sweating blood. Scientists have, from time to time, elaborated on this and said for a person to sweat blood, he would have to be under such intense fear and anxiety that the body has no other way to react. The condition is called hematidrosis and is most commonly found in prisoners approaching their execution.

There was, however, something much more significant in the agony Our Lord was undergoing than just fear of death. He said to Peter, James, and John that His soul was sorrowful, even to the point of death. The battle within Himself was so intense that in His humanity, He sought to escape it, to "let this cup pass from me" (Matt. xxvi:39).

The conflict in Our Blessed Lord, the drama, was not so much fear

of what lay ahead in His physical sufferings as it was the result of
the pain He felt in His heart, His soul, over sin. His humanity had
to contend with His divinity, creating an agony unmatched in the
history of the universe. His divine intellect comprehended all the
sin ever in the history of the race.

All the sins back to the beginning were present at this moment:
Adam, Cain, Sodom and Gomorrah, the sins of the world that
brought the Flood that only Noah and his family escaped, the
offerings to all the pagan gods, the betrayal and adultery of His
own people, the treachery of Judas. And all the future sins were
there as well: the abortions, broken marriages, the billions of illicit
sexual unions, the millions of rejections of Him by atheists, the
mockeries of His divinity by revolutionaries, the perversions of His
future priests, the silence of His Apostles and their successors
down through the ages, the Communists' slaughter of those who
proclaimed Him. All of it was now present in one moment and
presented to His humanity—and from this He recoiled. "My Father,
if it be possible, let this cup pass from me" (Matt. xvi:39).

But facing all this, there was still one last realization, one last
dynamic to face, and this one came not from the future, but from
eternity: that so many, the very ones for whom this agony was
being endured, would reject Him forever and ever. He would turn
from the horror and terror and ugliness of sin on His left, blood
rolling down from His forehead awaiting a crown of thorns, and
roll to His right and behold the mouth of Hell yawning to receive
billions of souls who would hate Him forever. The temptation must
have come: What good was His suffering? To what end?

So intense was the struggle, so severe the combat, that an angel
was sent to comfort Him. At no point in His earthly life did Our
Lord ever use His powers for His personal benefit, His ease, His
comfort. Yet on this occasion, so intense, so debilitating, so beyond
the simple fear of death was this agony that the assistance of an
angel was required. All of the sins of the world—hundreds of
billions of trillions of them, from past, present, and future—all
converged at this moment. Our Blessed Lord, completely isolated,

cut off from a single moment so He could be made present to all moments, contended with sin itself. One gigantic, explosive, nuclear moment of the entire history of sin collapsed into His soul in the Garden, and He cried aloud, "let this cup pass from me" (Matt. xxvi:39).

And then, the war of resistance, the clash between human and divine intellects, was resolved. The combat was over between God and sin—and sin lost. So complete was the defeat that the Savior would go out and confront it before it came to Him. He woke His sleeping Apostles and told them, "Rise, let us be going; see, my betrayer is at hand" (Matt. xxvi:46). The struggle is inevitable, the combat guaranteed. The fight must be fought. Pope Leo XIII stresses that we are born for this combat. Saint Paul sees his entire life in terms of fighting the fight. There is no escape from the war. Everyone is engaged. What is uncertain is the outcome in us as individuals. Our Lord forged the path in showing us what we must endure to achieve victory.

We must go out to the fight, engage the demon. This is what Our Lord does as He hears the tramp of footfall and catches glimpses of the flaming torches through the branches. Notice, He knew what was coming, but did not want His Apostles to flee. He woke them and said, "Rise, let us be going." He knew they would all abandon Him, yet He needed them to see with their own eyes what their eyes had not seen the past hour: the effect of sin. This was a supreme lesson to them. He would overcome by advancing on evil.

He does not turn away when Judas leans into His cheek. He accepts the mark of death on His Sacred Face from the lips of a devil. He meets it head on, for this is how battle is fought. No retreat. Attack, attack, attack! Then, addressing the crowd of thugs and mercenaries, He demands to know Whom they want. "Jesus of Nazareth," they respond. And again, meeting evil head on, stepping out to confront it, he declares, "I am He." And evil recoils at the challenge to its pride.

The mob had the numbers, the weapons, the torches, the guile, the audacity, the pride. Why fall back? Why not lunge forward? They had these earthly tactical advantages only because Our Lord refused to call down His twelve legions of angels. But the earlier struggle, the agony He had endured a few feet away from this confrontation, had given Him the strength to challenge them. He was the more powerful, and they sensed it. For all their clubs and chains, Jesus was stronger because He had resolved while sweating blood that sin should not win the day, that He would master it—and now the moment of conquest had arrived.

It was the hour of darkness, but only because He allowed it. He was quite possibly now looking into eternity again—only this time seeing the Catherines of Siena, the Francises of Assissi, the martyrs, the entirely heavenly cohort, and saying, "These you will not snatch from my hand. Take me and let the drama play until its end, for I shall not see another sunset, and when you mob see the next, you shall be redeemed." When He once again hid from them the glow of everlasting victory surrounding Him, He granted the darkness of the temporal moment permission to enter once again, and He allowed Himself to be bound and dragged away.

His Apostles ran away. Judas hanged himself. And Christ's angelic legions He commanded to sheathe their swords. This would be the way the Father willed it, and His will and the Father's are one.

Chapter 12

THE SECOND SORROWFUL MYSTERY:

The Scourging at the Pillar

Our Blessed Lord's Passion began with His agony in Gethsemane. There, the pain of His soul was expressed in His body as He sweat blood. Now, as He fell under the flogging of the Roman soldiers, professional executioners, the dynamic was reversed—the pain in His body would begin to impress itself in His soul.

Scourging by the Romans was always a precursor to crucifixion, but in this case it was a vain attempt on the part of Pontius Pilate to exact some pity from His accusers. It was the third attempt by Pilate to release Our Lord, over the loud objections of the Jewish leaders, whose cries he believed he must consider for reasons of state and the political order. They wanted Our Lord dead, publicly executed to quiet their own consciences. Pilate had a sense of this, however dimly, and believed that Jesus had committed no capital crime. He even judged, rightly, "I find no crime in him" (John xviii:38).

The conflict in this meditation centers on Pilate. He was conflicted between knowing an accused to be innocent and the will of the mob. In the balance lay political order, the status quo, the fear of lost careers, set against the dramatic background of a riot. He was the judge caught between a rock and a hard place, or so he styled his situation in his mind. Do the right or do the wrong with good intentions, however self-serving the intentions may be.

Even his wife Claudia weighed in. It was unprecedented for the wife of a Roman even to mention or attempt to influence the outcome of a trial. It was, in fact, a punishable offense. And yet, as Pilate sat there, perhaps hearing the sound of the scourge as it ripped away the Flesh of Our Lord, she was so resolute that even knowing she was breaking Roman law, she sent a message to Pilate to do the right thing. This was the first outside voice of reason that presented itself to Pilate. All others were pointing in one direction—to the Cross. Pilate's soul was disturbed, as are the souls of all spiritually hesitant. The gospels tell us that as the trial lingered on and various charges were hurled against Jesus, Pilate became "afraid" (John xix:8).

The one charge that shook him was on hearing from the leaders of the Sanhedrin that Jesus claimed to be the Son of God. As unsettling as that was, Pilate had a sense that there may be some kind of truth to it. On hearing that, he privately met with Jesus. He did not ask if the charge were true. That would be too direct. His mind was frazzled from being in the Divine Presence, something was electrified in his soul, his conscience was torn. This was nothing like anything he had encountered before.

He had a reputation for being ruthless in quelling unrest, swift to action, almost merciless. He let the Jews know who was boss, virtually crucifying at will. Yet in the case of Our Lord, something entirely different stirred within him he had never felt before. So when he heard the term "Son of God," his mind raced. Could this be true? Could this be a deity, or some kind of messenger from a deity? So he privately asked the leading question, "Where are you from?" (John xix:9).

Now consider for a moment the import of this question from Pilate's perspective. In one of his earlier ill-fated attempts to release Jesus, he had learned of His Galilean origin and therefore sent Him to Herod. Pilate, when asking this question, already knew Our Lord was from Galilee, so it is a revealing question, revealing of the mind of Pilate, when he asked Our Lord, "Where are you from?"

He was completely at combat within himself. He knew this Man was not like other men. Moreover, he had already proclaimed Him innocent, and yet for the sake of the crowd, and his own interests, He kept the trial going, seeking a way to appease the men yet not incur the wrath of a god. His conscience told him what to do, his wife told him what to do, and the public told him the opposite. He had come to the moment many do when confronted with the combat between self-interest and conscience, between pleasing the fickle mob and doing the right.

Meditate for a moment on the scene. Here stands a whipped Christ, crowned with thorns, flesh hanging from His body, a pool of blood accumulating at His feet. This kind of torture was certainly not new to Pilate. No one executed judgment more harshly and swiftly than the Romans. The picture of men reduced to a mass of bloodied flesh would have been something of a common scene. Yet here, through all that blood and horror, Pilate knew something else was at play, something that so disquieted him he wanted nothing to do with it.

In the end, he ordered the death of Our Lord. The scourging had failed to move the crowd, as justice always does for those who do not love it. How many times might Pilate have subjected Our Lord to the lash, to the flesh-ripping, iron-balled whips of the execution garrison of soldiers? He had tried three times before he ordered the scourging, neither of which had been successful, to free Our Lord: by declaring Him innocent, by sending Him to Herod, and by giving the crowd the choice of the murderous Barabbas instead of Jesus. For Pilate to subject Our Lord to the whip, to the scourge, was an act of injustice, for he knew Him to be innocent. This injustice cleared the way, conditioned him to commit the last and greatest injustice in condemning Him.

Scourging was a horrifying experience, as noted above, meted out to the condemned prior to crucifixion. The common scourge was a cat-of-nine tails—nine leather cords with small iron balls cut in half attached to each of the cords, all gathered together at the point of a handle. The iron balls had ragged edges, like dull razors, capable of inflicting extreme pain owing to the great damage they caused in ripping chunks of skin and flesh from the bone. The scourge was not a whip, but a flesh-removal device, exposing bone and causing tremendous amounts of blood loss. It was a "warm-up" to crucifixion, a subduing of the condemned, to lessen any resistance he may offer during the march to his death and subsequent nailing to the wood.

For Pilate to have subjected Our Lord to this was a grave sin. Yet he ultimately did it out of self-interest. True, he may have wanted to soften the opposition to Our Lord by presenting Him to the crowds as a beaten pulp who would never again cause controversy by His teachings, but He also had His own interest at heart—trying to clear his conscience by not ordering the execution. Perhaps he was playing a mental game of the lesser of two evils. "After all," he may have mused, "better for him to fall under the scourge than die on the cross." And even more quietly, "better for me that I somehow satisfy this bloodthirsty crowd than face some career-threatening riot." He sought the compromise, the much-heralded "common ground." Yet common ground initiatives prove fruitless when it is truth that is sacrificed to achieve the compromise.

So with Our Lord standing there, fresh from the scourging, and Pilate afraid at the whole series of events, he asked Our Lord, "Where are you from?" And Jesus gave him no answer, for there was nothing else to say. Pilate already knew the man was innocent; what would knowing His divine origin do, what part would it play in Pilate's following his conscience? Is it justice to ignore your conscience and condemn the innocent, as long as he is not a god or a messenger of the gods? Pilate knew what the truth of the situation was on a merely natural level—he had already declared it multiple times.

He had put an innocent man to the whip, the flesh-tearing scourge for political expediency, and now, no matter how much he knew the truth, he refused to act on it. That set him up to, again, reject his own conscience and order the crucifixion. But there is one thing worth noting, as the judgment was being leveled against the scourged, thorn-crowned innocent Man: Pilate did what many do when they have rejected the inner truth, the barking conscience. He passed the responsibility of his sin on to others, carried out symbolically by the washing of his hands. "I am innocent of this righteous man's blood" (Matt. xxvii:24). Pilate was no more innocent than Judas or the Sanhedrin. And no amount of water could erase his complicity in deicide.

The leaders knew in their conscience that to bring Our Lord to Pilate was evil. And Pilate knew in his conscience to condemn Our Lord, after a scourging, was also evil. Evil builds on evil, and the process can only be stopped when one adheres to one's conscience. This is why the battle, the combat that arises in the soul of every Catholic, must be settled according to conscience, and a conscience that is aligned with Truth. Pilate, no doubt, sentenced many, many men to death. The death sentence of Our Lord, however, is the only ruling he is remembered for, and because he betrayed his conscience and chose to please the crowd, the echoes of his actions have been repeated by millions of voices down through the millennia: "He suffered under Pontius Pilate . . . ."

Chapter 13

THE THIRD SORROWFUL MYSTERY:

The Crowning with Thorns

In this meditation, let us consider the conflict, the confrontation between good and evil in the soldiers of the garrison—for every man is capable of torturing his enemies, real or perceived, given sufficient anger. The soldiers of the garrison were the professional executioners. They did this for a living, which is why the spurious charge by some odd religions that Jesus survived the crucifixion and therefore did not rise from the dead is ludicrous. These soldiers were good at what they did.

The entire Roman justice system was based on the ability to mete out what was punished and to execute orders to their completion. Consider the siege of Jerusalem for two years before its final destruction in 70 A.D. Each legion, each garrison, each detachment, each unit was charged with the complete following of orders. If Jesus was sentenced to die by crucifixion at the hands of executioners, then He was executed.

Consider also that these men woke up every morning and went about their duties in workmanlike fashion. They scourged people, drove nails through men's hands and feet, pulled down corpses from crosses by chopping off their feet, and tossed the corpses into a hole of rotting, fetid flesh. These men were well accustomed to pain and agony, for they inflicted it on others. It was their stock and trade. They were, to use an informal phrase, where the buck stopped. They were the final link in the chain of Roman justice.

To be delivered into the hands of the executioners of Rome was a frightful thing. Consider that Pilate ordered the scourging, but he did not order what followed: the mockery, thorns, beating, spitting. All of that was done in a "freelance" fashion. Who knows? Maybe the Romans hadn't seen a prisoner for a few days and were especially eager to discharge their boredom.

There is much to consider in the tortures and humiliations going on in Pilate's hall. Let us consider the combat between man and God, for that is what is occurring in these sufferings, with each of the tortures able to be seen in terms of conflict.

'And they stripped him and put a scarlet robe upon him" (Matt. xxvii:28). Our Blessed Lord had been dragged into the hall fresh from His scourging, naked or nearly naked. Then He had clothing thrown over Him—a robe of royal scarlet. Two dynamics were accomplished in this act: the humiliation of mockery intended by the soldiers, and the further unseen humiliation of Our Lord's being "covered" as though He were a sinner, as our first parents were covered as a result of sin.

Adam and Eve were clothed because of sin. Prior to that, their innocence left them in a state that never required clothing. But the sin of Adam and Eve caused the rebellion of the flesh against the spirit and produced a general feeling of shame. All this combined with their expulsion from Eden and their consequent exile imposed on mankind the necessity of external dress. Dress is both the punishment of the sinner as well as identifier of his sinfulness. Our Lord, being purely innocent, had no need of clothing on His own, but chose to bear the garments of sin. He had had His tunic made by Our Blessed Mother torn from Him for the scourging. From the hands of the pure Immaculate to the body of pure Innocence, this was the only garment fitting for Him, for which the soldiers would cast lots.

In its place, a stained, worn-out, red cloak, possibly from the back of a soldier's horse, draped over Him—a sign to us that He accepted the "dress of sin." Origen made special comment on the draping of the cloak when he said, *Suscipiens Dominus clamydem coccineam in se, sanguinem mundi, idest peccata suscepit* (roughly translated, "The Lord bears upon Himself a crimson cloak stained by the blood of the world from its sin").

Next came the reed placed into His hand, again a symbol of the combat necessary to overcome Hell. They "put a reed in his right hand" (Matt. xxvii:29). The soldiers meant it in derision, a scepter for the King of the Jews, but again there is the double dynamic: The reed is the perfect symbol of our human weakness, emptiness, and inconstancy. It has no real substance, nothing sturdy; it blows about at the slightest wind or breeze. If not in the hands of Our Lord, our nature is all this, we are all this. We succumb to every temptation, every breeze of seduction. But in His hands we are made strong.

The Fathers of the Church saw the connection immediately. Saint Ambrose says, "Our Lord has taken the reed of our humanity in His hand in order to hinder the frailty of our fallen nature from being tossed by every wind of false doctrine and to render it firm and steady by the truth of faith and solid by the fullness of virtuous works." The combat is to place ourselves into Our Lord's hands and be transformed from reeds into scepters.

When it comes to the crown of thorns, there is something to consider in the first place. The origin of thorns is from Original Sin. When Our Lord was crowned with them, He was truly accepting a crown of sin in our place. Here in the city of David of whom He was a descendant, in the hall of Pilate, He received His crown. He had been anointed King in the waters of the Jordan, and now three years later came the coronation. The thorns were one of God's punishments, a curse for sin, and therefore God's justice had to be satisfied by thorns being born. *In corona spinea maledictum solvit antiquum* (roughly translated, "The ancient curse that was paid for with a crown of thorns").

The fourth outrage Our Lord suffered at the hands of the executioners were the mocking and insults. "And kneeling before him they mocked him, saying, 'Hail, King of the Jews!' And they spat upon him, and took the reed and struck him on the head" (Matt. xxvii:29–30). This passage reveals that in addition to thorns, robe, and reed, four different mockeries were made of Our Lord. He was derided by their kneeling and bowing before Him; they feigned lauds for Him by saluting Him as King of the Jews; they struck His head with the reed; and they spat on Him. Each of these actions speaks to daily conflict of man in relation to God.

The first mockery can be seen as signifying pagans' worship of false gods. They give Jesus fake worship. But while their actions were fake, the object of their actions was the one true God. In receiving their false worship, God was able to expiate for all the worship of pagans and idolaters. Such people now had a path cleared for them by God to engage in true worship.

The second mockery was the derision of the title "King of the Jews." Yet He *was* King of the Jews, so once again, as in their fake worship, they were actually correct in calling Him this. The derision He endured, like the path being cleared for the pagans with their false worship, clears the path for the Jews to accept Him as King and Messiah. They had rejected Him earlier this day and proclaimed they had no King but Caesar. Through this humiliation, He suffered for them, that they might return to Him, as they will before the end of the world.

The third insult was being struck with the reed across His head crowned with thorns—a sign of heretics. Heretics strike at the head of Christ when they strike at Peter, the visible head of the Body of Christ. The way had to be made clear for them to return from their insolence and heresy, and so Our Lord receives the blows against His own Sacred Head to expiate for their sins.

And the final sacrilege is being spat on in the face. This signifies the Catholics who reject Christ in the face. The aspect of the face is crucial because, as St. Gregory notes, we know a person by his face. So this comes from those who know Our Blessed Lord. They know Him and spit on Him. Their example leads others into sin. These need a way back to Our Lord, and He provides it by allowing His Holy Face to become a target for the spittle of the soldiers.

Chapter 14

THE FOURTH SORROWFUL MYSTERY:

The Carrying of the Cross

In this mystery of the Rosary, we can meditate on the literal reality of what Our Blessed Lord commanded us to do: Pick up the cross and carry it. Here is spiritual combat in its fullest expression. The crosses of life are the only road to Heaven. There is no path to the tomb in the Garden that does not pass through Golgotha. And Golgotha cannot be reached without carrying the cross along the *Via Dolorosa*, the Way of Sorrows. It is on this path that a man is forged and his eternal destiny achieved or lost. That so many lose it makes it indeed the Way of Sorrows. The sons of God are tried along this path, made perfect. It is here they suffer the humiliations, the rejection of their former popularity.

As Our Lord dragged His bleeding body under the weight of the Cross step by painful step, He no doubt saw some of the faces and heard some of the same voices that a few days earlier were singing hosannas. But the mob is fickle. It cannot be a reliable gauge. What is lauded one day is cursed the next. Our Lord knew this. He entered Jerusalem and rode to the Temple knowing that only a few sunsets lay between Him and His final journey out of the city—only this time, He would be the beast of burden, physically and spiritually.

It was the normal routine along the way to execution to have a man in the lead blowing a trumpet to clear the path and then a herald announcing the charge against the criminal and proclaiming his name. Our Blessed Lord was leaving the world the same way He came in. Angels had blown their trumpets over those shepherds keeping night watch over their sheep in the hills surrounding Bethlehem, and John the Baptist led the way of introduction by announcing the Lamb of God. And this is what He truly was now: the Lamb being led to the slaughter.

It was also customary to hang a sign around the neck of the condemned on which was written his name and crime. The point would be well understood by onlookers that mercy was a rare commodity if you offended the emperor. And because He was officially executed for treason, it would be all the more fitting that the charge of His being a King should accompany Him to the Cross and then the grave.

The lesson from Our Lord's slow march to His place of execution is our duty to do the same. So exhausted and nearly dead was He at the beginning of the trail that a man was pressed into service to assist with the Cross, lest the Criminal were to cheat His executioners out of their fun on Golgotha. While the Cross may be ours, and we all have them, we need help with them. Simon of Cyrene was Our Lord's help.

However much he initially protested or resented being drafted and strong-armed by the execution squad, an enormous impression was burnt into his psyche, for not all that much later, his two sons, Rufus and Alexander, are mentioned as pillars of the Church. What begins as a heavy weight and undesirable duty can become the means of salvation for those around us.

As unwilling as he was at the beginning, he became something of a "sacrament" to Our Blessed Lord. He helped Him get to the point of dying the death that glorified God, and at the end of the day, that is the entire reason for the sacraments: so that at our last breath, we may have spent a lifetime preparing to say, "Father, into Your hands I commend My spirit." Say that, and you will behold the Beatific Vision. Die as the bad thief, and you will behold the face of Satan.

There is a certain quality needed in how we carry the cross. Along the way, Our Blessed Lord broke His silence, a silence He had kept since refusing to give answer to Pilate's frightened inquiry regarding His origins. He would not speak to the unjust except to offer them conversion, but He would offer a correction to the innocent and misinformed: the weeping women of Jerusalem.

What we learn of combat in the suffering of Our Lord that we are to forge into the armor of our struggle is this: The sufferings can never be about us. The comfort He provided to the women was not comfort at all, but an outward glancing from His own agonies to a concern over what was going to befall them and their children. He gave them a warning: Ignore My Cross, and focus on your own.

He did not ask for comfort from them; in fact, He rejected it. What He wanted from them was to realize the need to repent, to tell those around them to turn to Him as escape from the coming doom of Jerusalem. He became a model, the exemplar for every cross-carrying Catholic to lay aside the difficulties of their own struggle from their minds and focus on souls. Jerusalem was doomed. He had foretold it, and its destruction would be a figure, a type of the end of the world.

This is what cross-bearers must point to among their loved ones, family, friends, everyone in their world: the announcement that a tragic end is awaiting in future history, of those days yet to unfold, and they must prepare, now. And the preparation will be made by carrying the cross. Life is full of crosses, but if they are not picked up, embraced, carried, they are nothing more than travails with no power to transform. A man who has grown weary of his wife—this only merits the wood of a cross when he loves her all the more. If he throws her aside, leaves his cross on the roadside, then he is not fit for Heaven.

The wife who no longer feels fulfilled in romantic fantasies she once applied to her husband, who rejects the monotony of matrimony and leaves her husband, leaves her path to salvation. For it is not possible to walk the path without the cross. The cross is the cost of admission to the Way of Sorrows. Without it, you will be plunged into even greater sorrows.

Our Lord tells the women, "Daughters of Jerusalem, do not weep for me, but weep for yourselves and for your children" (Luke xxiii: 28). Because Jerusalem did not recognize the moment of its salvation, it would be destroyed, as will all people who fail the moment. No one is spared the Divine Justice. The Divine Mercy is that He allows us to walk in imitation of His carrying of the Cross to participate in our salvation. Anyone who does not has forfeited the mercy and will inherit the justice.

The annals of history reveal that during the siege of Jerusalem by Titus and his Tenth Legion, they surrounded the city and cut off all food and water supplies going into the city. They then slowly built ramparts to breach the walls; the effort took a couple of years. Inside the city walls, starvation seized the people. And in fulfillment of Our Lord's words about weeping for their children, historians report that mothers, driven mad with hunger, boiled their children in cisterns and ate their flesh.

There is no way around the sufferings of this life. But those sufferings can become sanctified if they are attached to the Cross, carried for the sake of salvation. This takes courage—the sort of courage a soldier must summon while running headlong into battle. Courage is the overcoming of fear, not the absence of it. The Cross must be accepted with courage and determination, even when—especially when—we know that our final destiny is to arrive on Golgotha with it in tow.

Chapter 15

THE FIFTH SORROWFUL MYSTERY:

The Crucifixion and Death of Our Lord

There is no greater contradiction than the Cross. Even its physical layout is a contradiction—one beam horizontal, the other vertical. And a cross makes no sense without a sacrifice laid upon it.

The interior struggle to present ourselves for crucifixion is immense, yet each of us must mount the gibbet, as Our Blessed Lord did. As Venerable Archbishop Fulton Sheen used to say, "No love ever mounts to a higher level without death to a lower one."

This must be the calling of every Catholic—an embrace of death, not for its own sake, but for the sake of transformation of self. Death is the wages of sin and we all spend a lifetime dying, undergoing death.

Perhaps it is the mercy of a generous, yet just, God that He permits us little "rehearsals" for our physical deaths. As we age, life becomes more burdensome for us compared to the physical freedoms of youth. As we travel through life, the sincere man will recognize various humiliations that befall him and the consequent need to change, to transform, as little deaths.

Our Lord, of course, needed no such "training" or "practice" for death for He was perfect and never sinned. But we do. We need to die to ourselves, die to the sins we have embraced that have marred our souls and so disfigured the *Imago Dei*, the image of God, in which we were created. True, Original Sin had already begun the process, but we have spent a lifetime in personal sin, advancing the defacing of our souls.

Sin kills. But along the way, it isolates. It most especially isolates us from God. And what is death other than isolation, for no one dies with us. We die completely alone, cut off from everyone we ever knew on earth. No one undergoes our death for us—each must experience his own.

For the poor sinner who dies isolated from God, consider the horror for him. He may have bragged in life about there being no God, or been indifferent to the reality of God, but at the moment of death, he arrives at his personal Waterloo. But for these too Our Lord endured the Crucifixion. It was them most especially over whom He cried out when He prayed, "My God, my God, why hast thou forsaken me?" (Matt. xxvii:46).

There was not a pain on earth that was not pulled down on the suffering Christ and felt in His body, mind, or soul. This includes the pain of isolation, of the atheist, of those mocking Him at the foot of the Cross. He knew what tortures awaited them in the future owing to their rejection of Him, but He still needed to feel their future pain in His present.

Divine Love knows no bounds, and the challenge that is laid out for His followers is to love as He loved—sacrificially. This is the heart of spiritual combat—the war at its most fundamental level. The battle with all its humiliations hurled at you for being a follower of Christ, a loyal son of the Church—herein lies the immense challenge to the soul.

And there is no turning back from this without enduring everlasting humiliation. Having arrived at our personal Golgotha, a person cannot come down from the Cross, as the passersby and Christ's enemies, even the soldiers, tempted Him to. Giving up the Cross means giving up love—love of souls, rightly ordered love of self, and most importantly, love of God.

The place of the skull is a lonely place; there is little solace there. There is pain, mockery, insult, indifference, lack of compassion, temptation to abandon the gibbet. And there is betrayal. One wonders if Our Lord might have been able to see in the distance the body of Judas swinging from a tree—the same Judas He had dipped His bread in the plate with less than twenty-four hours earlier.

Or could He see the Apostles cowering behind some rocks or boulders, safe from the line of sight of the Roman executioners? They could not bring themselves to die for Him, even though Peter had, the night before, made an oath He would do so. Did their cowardice near Golgotha remind Him further of His isolation in the Garden, when He twice turned to them in His most excruciating hour on earth, while they snored? It is one thing to be misunderstood and rejected by your enemies; it is quite another to be ignored in your suffering by your intimates.

He was alone, isolated in the Garden. All He had before His moment of resolve was a conversation with the Father, which brought Him no consolation. He would have to drink the full measure of the Father's wrath, and no one else could do it. The last bitter dregs of the chalice would in fact be the isolation. To whom could He turn to try and explain it all? Who could grasp the complete picture? For the time of His isolation, pinned to a tree between Heaven and Earth, there was no one. Even His questioning cry to the Father of why He had abandoned Him was isolated, not understood. In fact, it was misunderstood by His enemies, who thought He was calling on Elijah.

A few lingering souls at the foot of the Cross were provided to ease His misery. Yet even here, consider the level of sorrow, the depth of feeling that would have passed between Our Lord and His Blessed Mother as She looked up at Him, and He down at Her—the most bittersweet moment in human history—She the Mother of Sorrows, He the Suffering Servant of prophecy, yet at the same time the New Eve and the New Adam, God and the "Woman" He had prophesied of in Eden all those millennia ago.

The suffering was not without effect. Despite nature covering its face and the earth rocking beneath them, responding to deicide, the suffering was not without merit. At the end of the world, on the Last Day, the saddest epitaph of human history will not be the needless suffering, but the wasted suffering. Because of the Cross, all suffering now has the potential for merit. It must be brought to Calvary and placed there at the first crucifix, a living crucifix. This is the heart of spiritual warfare. Only God can transform evil into good, draw out redemption and salvation from acts of selfishness. Our Lord was on the Cross because Pilate did not want to upset Caesar. Our Lord was on the Cross because the Jews did not want to upset the status quo of awaiting a Messiah, and all that came with it.

Nonredemptive suffering is wasted suffering. But redemptive suffering transforms—because no love ever mounts to a higher level without death to a lower one. Spouses know this instinctively. When the vows are exchanged, the old self dies and a new self emerges. Calvary was the nuptial bed of Our Lord and His Bride. "For this reason a man shall leave his father and mother and be joined to his wife, and the two shall become one flesh" (Eph. v:31).

Here at the place of the skull, Christ wedded Himself to His Bride, and the two became one flesh. He had left His Father and Mother, and history would forever be changed—a race would be redeemed. Before the Incarnation, the Second Person was not yet Redeemer in the order of time. The suffering of Christ in a sense transformed Him, and when unredeemed man was united to the Redeemer, the two became one flesh. Those who would cling to Him, cleave to Him, would be His spouse forever, for what God has joined together, let no man put asunder.

But the Beloved must also undergo the suffering for the Lover. The enemy that the Lover faced the Beloved must also contend with, do battle with, and vanquish. Love is proven in sacrifice, the sacrifice of combat, for this is our identity as His followers. The Cross is the path, it is where the marriage is consummated, and without the Cross, without the fight, the struggle, the combat, the clash, the contradiction, our love fails. But when love triumphs, new life emerges. The spouses are transformed into parents. Even there on Golgotha, with a tiny, nascent, embryonic Church witnessing the agony in the persons of Our Blessed Mother, John, Magdalen, John's mother, and a couple of others, the next generation was being born. Dismas, the good thief, would enter Paradise before the sun set. A Roman guard, the head of the execution squad, would declare the divinity of the executed. Nature gave its testimony in the darkened sky and splitting of rocks. Nothing would ever be the same.

As Our Lord commanded death to come to Him so that it might serve as the chariot for Him to come home to His Father, He let rip the cry of victory that all was consummated. Indeed it was consummated. Such is the power of the Cross, even to unite Heaven and fallen earth. This is why it must be picked up and carried, as He commanded.

As one looks about the Church today, it is easy to be reminded of the reality that shook St. Paul about the Cross. He was consider-ing the reality of a spectacularly failed mission to Athens where he had tried to out-clever and over-philosophize the Greeks. He had held the Cross in reserve and drained his preaching of its content and power. He resolved from that point forward never to preach anything except Christ crucified. He had made a dreadful miscalculation in trying to meet the Greeks on their own terms. He did not let the power of the Cross transform, radiate to his listeners. Instead, he buried it. He buried it, and without its power, he lost to them, for no man on his own can preach salvation.

He learned that day that only the Cross can save. No amount of Madison Avenue marketing and clever slogans can convert a man's heart. And he also learned that only those who are crucified can preach. Only the weak can be captured and nailed to a tree. But in that weakness, as St. Paul said, they are made strong. A key component in the spiritual combat is the recognition of our weakness—and not just some generic "I'm not perfect" admission that merits a man nothing, for the whole race sings that song, but an actual understanding that without God, you can do nothing. The current crisis of the Church is the same crisis that too many individuals face, for the Church is, in one dynamic, a collection of individuals—and that crisis is a crisis of faith, faith in the Cross. We are afraid to own it, preach it, live it, and be nailed to it. This is true of the hierarchy as well as of the laity. Authentic salvation cannot be preached from any pulpit other than the Cross. On that Cross the world will ridicule you, mock you, offer you drugged wine to shut you up. You will be misunderstood, rejected, have your possessions taken from you to be divided among others.

But there is no other place and no other way to embrace the Cross than to talk about salvation, which means damnation as well. How can we preach a Savior if we do not preach about that from which He is saving us? The world has no desire to hear spiritual pabulum from Christ's followers. It does not want to hear guitars and watered-down, "emotional" catechesis—the world is already awash, drowning in that, and the world does a better job of it.

No one will be converted without the redemptive suffering of Christ experienced in our own bones, hearts, souls, minds. And while the sad truth is that most will still reject the message, demand a miracle, or pass by indifferent, the suffering will bring about salvation for those thieves and soldiers who otherwise would have been lost.

Each of us must take up our cross of isolation, repudiation, and torment and die so that others may live. And in that death, we are prepared for resurrection.

Chapter 16

THE FIRST GLORIOUS MYSTERY:

The Resurrection

A point of combat, of contest, to meditate on while considering the Resurrection would be the struggle of faith. And a distinction should be made between natural faith and supernatural faith.

Natural faith is what every human being possesses and acts on a thousand times a day. It is an expectation of how things should be: The car key will start the engine; the fire will heat the meal; the tap will run the water. From the moment a man wakes up and places his feet on the floor, having, of course, an expectation that it is there, he exercises natural faith.

Supernatural faith is of an entirely different kind and magnitude. It does not come to us naturally. It is infused. It is the theological virtue that has God as its end, which allows us to believe what God has told us is true because He has said it.

One of the strangest things to consider in history is just how sorely lacking in faith all of our Blessed Lord's intimates were that He would actually rise from the dead. The Sanhedrin believed in the possibility more than the Apostles and His followers. Only Our Blessed Mother knew because only She possessed supernatural faith, as well as hope and charity.

Our faith is lacking greatly these days. It is the single cause most responsible for the destruction that has occurred within the walls of Fortress Catholicism. The events surrounding Our Lord's glorious emergence from the tomb illustrate this very clearly. We may ask ourselves: When Our Lord stepped out, who was present to greet Him? Frightened Roman soldiers so terrified at the sight of the angel that they fell to the ground like dead men. What a sad commentary for the first Easter, that no one from the Church was present to witness the victory—only those nearly lifeless guards who would later erase their memories in exchange for a huge sum of money from the Jewish leaders.

And present in spirit, in the spirit of anticipation, were the Jewish leaders themselves. It would not be prudent to presume their sole motive for wanting the Roman guards posted was to prevent a theft in the dead of night by the Apostles. Somewhere down deep, they had admitted the possibility that He might indeed rise from the grave. They knew He had raised Lazarus. They knew He had raised Jairus' daughter. They heard the reports too that the widow's son had been restored to life as the funeral procession was bearing him to his grave, and that he had been given back to his widowed mother. No doubt, many of these claims had been quietly investigated by them.

They knew Who He was, without understanding what He was. So the possibility of some kind of resurrection was not without foundation in their minds. Our Lord anticipated their partial belief when He said that even if someone were to come back from the dead, there would be those who would not believe. Their presence in spirit at the tomb was not based on hope, and certainly not on charity, the supernatural companions of faith, but rather on a natural faith, that while they could not quite understand or grasp the significance of a bodily resurrection, they understood the implications to the status quo and their own careers. So half out of fear for their careers and half out of a dim acceptance that it might happen, they petitioned Pilate for a guard at the tomb and for the tomb to be sealed.

While meditating on the Resurrection, try to draw into your mind the responses of the Chief Priest and his cohorts when the guards came and told them what had happened. It was precisely what they had feared and quietly anticipated, however dimly. Their natural faith was enough to motivate their actions after His death. But let us also consider in our meditation the complete lack of faith, both natural and of course supernatural, among Our Blessed Lord's intimates. There was none; it was absent. This is evidenced from the moment He was taken down from the Cross. No one, except Our Lady, had even the slightest amount of faith that they would see Him again.

This is obvious from how they prepared His sacred body, even rushing owing to the approaching Sabbath. If Joseph of Arimathea and Nicodemus had the slightest hope or faith that Our Lord was going to burst out of the tomb on the third day, they would not have been so careful in wrapping and anointing His body.

So too the women who had been so closely devoted to Him did not have faith. They were approaching the tomb to complete the anointing that had been cut short by the Sabbath. That the great stone rolled in front of the tomb would have been tossed aside by an angel was never even contemplated by them. In fact, just the opposite was the focus of their discussion as it dawned on them that they couldn't get in the tomb because of the huge boulder. "Who will roll away the stone for us from the door of the tomb?" (Mark xvi:3).

Even the initial evidence of a resurrection did not move them to credulity. At no moment during this early dawn did they recall the words, the promise of our Blessed Lord that on the third day He would rise again. His enemies had heard those same words and considered them carefully—carefully enough to at least post a guard. Yet to His followers, it was as though He had never spoken them, so far from their minds were they.

On the great perplexing question facing the Church in Her individual members today, this one combative reality stands out regarding the central point of Catholicism: that on that first Easter, the believers did not believe, and the unbelievers did. So too as the story circulated, the Apostles rejected it. So too did the disciples on the road to Emmaus. They admitted to the concealed Lord that they had heard the fanciful tale, but no one had seen anything. The Early Church needed proof, visible, tangible, "reach out your hands and touch it" proof.

In their defense, from a strictly human level, they had been through a lot in the preceding sixty hours: a traitor in their midst, their own denials and betrayals and unwillingness to stand by Our Lord, the associated feelings of guilt and remorse that had to overwhelm each one of them, the sadness and grief of having not only betrayed or deserted and denied this Man Whom they loved so dearly, but the harsh reality that it was all over.

Whatever they had imagined or hoped things to be was all over. They would never again be able to hear His voice. He was dead. He had spoken of a Kingdom, with them seated on thrones. He had called them friends. There was a mix of grief, confusion, hopelessness, and fear—fear that the authorities would now come seek them out. They had escaped three nights earlier in the Garden, but the possibility existed that they would be next.

So it is understandable from the perspective of fallen human nature that the Apostles were so distressed and shaken that news that He was alive was too hard to hear. Could they allow their minds for just an instant to accept the possibility? Could they hope? Could their darkness be dispelled? What if they did allow it, the possibility, the consideration? What if they built themselves back up, only to be dashed on the rocks of reality?

No matter how deep the pain was at this moment, the thought of having hope ripped from them was too much. They had lost faith. They had not sufficient charity. They could not venture the emotional gamble of having hope destroyed as well. So they did what every fallen human being would do: They chose not to put themselves in a position to be hurt further. They rejected the news. So grief-stricken were they that Our Lord knew He would have to prove it to them, and in convincing order. For the disciples walking to Emmaus, He had first proven it to their minds and then to their bodies. It was the opposite for His Apostles: first the body, then the minds. All of a sudden He was there before them.

Meditate on this moment carefully. Place yourself in the Upper Room, a room of sorrows. It was the last place they had any intimacy with Our Lord. It would be the first place they would regain it. You are talking with Thaddeus or Andrew, lamenting, looking to console each other where no consolation can be found, excepting that of shared misery as at the funeral of a loved one, for misery truly does love company.

You then sense something inexplicable behind you. You see a look of amazement on the face of Andrew. He rubs his eyes. You turn and disbelieve your own senses. You had believed them readily enough two days earlier when you watched and heard from a distance the hammer pound onto the nails. You believed them when you heard the cry, "It is finished." But now, you do not believe.

The Gospel account tells us they believed Him to be a ghost. It was the second time we hear of the Apostles denying Our Lord's fleshy presence, and both owing to a lack of faith. The Apostles were incredulous. This couldn't be real. Also consider in your meditation all that had transpired up to this moment: Mary Magdalene had earlier crashed through the door with the news, and later in the day, two disciples likewise had run straight to the band of mourners with the news that they had heard and seen Him, and that He had set their hearts on fire. Peter had been visited by Him privately earlier as well. They had known from their long three years with Him that He had told them this many times. They had heard Him prophesy about His resurrection. Did not those memories receive even an instant of acknowledgment? Did not one Apostle, on hearing these repeated claims throughout this third day, not say to the others, "Maybe it's true?"

Another point to consider is that guilt prevented them from accepting the reality. With the exception of John, all of them had deserted Him. And yet here are reports from multiple sources that He is risen. He has been seen. Perhaps playing over in their minds was the thought that He was risen but was so angry at them for their desertions He would not come to them. He could appear to Mary Magdalene, for she had not abandoned Him. But them? In either case, it was still too impossible to be true. If He were risen, they might have to confront their guilt. If He weren't and they allowed themselves to believe, they would plunge themselves into even greater sadness.

Such was the emotional, mental, psychological chaos in the minds of His friends. But suddenly, their Divine Master was there, not calling them to account for their sin of desertion but for their failing of faith. I am no ghost. See, plunge your fingers and hands into My wounds. Give Me food.

His first words to them were, "Peace be with you" (John xx:19). He could have said something much different, they feared. In their minds and hearts, they considered He might have demanded an accounting of their fleeing from His cause in the Garden the previous Thursday. He might have asked why He saw only one of them at the foot of the Cross. Where were the other ten?

No. He brought a word of peace. There would be time for making good later. For every one of them not at the foot of the Cross, martyrdom awaited down the road, a martyrdom that not only allowed them to witness to what, or rather Whom, they had once run away from in fear, but also to give them the opportunity to prove their love for Him in the greatest way possible.

Little by little, their minds came to accept what the senses were feeding them. They touched, heard, watched Him eat. They were so overjoyed they could now not believe because of joy. At first they did not believe because of lack of faith; now they were incredulous owing to joy. In this same room not seventy-two hours earlier Our Lord had told them He was going away from them for a short time and they would be sad. Then He would return to them, and that joy no one would take from them.

We must overcome our failing faith. These men, the first to reject the news of the Resurrection, would soon receive the charge to go convince first those who had lobbied for His death, and then a pagan empire, of what they themselves had rejected.

Chapter 17

THE SECOND GLORIOUS MYSTERY:

The Ascension

The time had come for Our Lord to proceed to Heaven, to sit at the right hand of the Father, not so He could abandon His followers, but so He could complete them. They were in need of the Holy Spirit to begin and continue the mission He was about to give them.

The forty days between the Resurrection and the Ascension of Our Blessed Lord were days of formation. He made eleven recorded appearances in these days, but chances are He made many more than the number recorded. They did not know it yet, but they were being prepared to continue His work. So He deliberately and gently formed them, prepared them for what lay ahead.

They needed to have a solid understanding of Who He was, how He was prepared for from the time of the Fall. They needed to understand He was the seed of the Woman from Genesis Who would crush the head of the serpent. Everything recorded and written and prophesied about Him they needed to grasp and burn into their memories.

For the forty days Our Blessed Lord was the Teacher, in addition to being Savior. His primary work during the years leading up to and encompassing the Passion was as Savior, not primarily as Teacher. Now, for this small period of engagement, He became Teacher to His band of followers. He explained to them everything, much of it not written down, as one of the receivers of the information—St. John—testifies to in his own Gospel.

That it took forty days, perhaps—we can imagine many classes each day—proves the multitude of facts, knowledge, and data they were hearing. They were absorbing and processing, like students in a classroom hearing isolated pieces of information. They would not fully connect all the information, integrate it into a coherent whole, until ten days after Our Lord's feet left the earth. But for now, this was the design of Heaven, the blueprint for what would be built after His leaving.

The accumulation of knowledge is necessary for the followers of Christ. This is true for two main reasons: one, to combat the lies and misinformation the enemy spreads; and two, to increase in holiness, or rather to be readied to increase in holiness. An ancient maxim from the realms of philosophy is "You cannot give what you do not have." Participation in the life of Christ requires knowledge of Him. But knowledge of Him must, in a material world of time and space, begin with knowledge about Him.

After knowledge is gained, sufficient knowledge, then that knowledge can be the springboard to knowledge of Him. An artist must first gather his paints, acquire the canvas, mix the colors, treat the canvas, before his artistry can come to life. Every great deed requires preparation. Every block of marble must first be treated before being honed into a statue. Every lump of coal must first be cleaned before being subjected to the crush of being formed into a diamond. This is why Holy Mother Church has always entreated Her sons to learn, to apply themselves to the rigors of the intellect. If the ground is not properly prepared, how can the seed take root and grow?

The Rosary is an instruction, a review of salvation history. It is a school, very much like the school Our Lord enrolled the Apostles in during those forty days of formation. The Rosary is a school of formation, the condensed course of the forty days. And the classes began immediately in earnest on that first Easter Sunday night and continued for the semester of forty days. Like that first Easter, the Rosary begins with a call to faith. On the blessed crucifix is declared the faith: "I believe in One God . . . ."

Our Lord exacted this act of faith from the Apostles in the Upper

Room on Easter night. Nothing was possible without the preceding act of faith, however halting, unsure, incompletely grasped. It made no difference to Our Lord. All He needed was the mustard seed of faith, and He would develop it into the "largest of all shrubs."

So lacking faith whereby they dismissed out of hand reports of His bodily resurrection, He went to them. They eventually believed because they saw, but they first had to overcome their lack of faith in even their own senses. Even the smallest of faith can give way to greater faith, but it must be made present. Once the tuition of faith was paid, the work could begin. He turned to the script of His life, pre-announced in the Sacred Scriptures.

"'[E]verything written about me in the law of Moses and the prophets and the psalms must be fulfilled.' Then he opened their minds to understand the scriptures" (Luke xxiv:44–50). They did not as yet completely comprehend all they were hearing, nor the need for it in future days. But for these first forty days, they sat attentively.

We must do this. We are their descendants in the Faith. What they passed on to us originates with God. Notice He did not send them out during this incubation period. They would spend the rest of their mortal years presenting Our Lord to those who would largely reject Him. No, this time was a spiritual boot camp, a time to be with their Divine Master, because days were coming when He would no longer be an earthly companion to them as He had previously been. This was the time of preparation, of tilling, of planting.

And then, with no notice, it was over. The clock had run out, and Our Blessed Lord's direct, hands-on work among them was completed. They now understood much in the light and brilliance of the Resurrection. They were ready for graduation. They had not passed with a perfect score, and this is important to note. Our Lord prepared them for the work of saving souls, but they were still thinking in terms of an earthly salvation.

He was instructing them in the business of the forgiveness of sins. It was His first action before the body of Apostles on Easter Sunday night. "If you forgive the sins of any, they are forgiven; if you retain the sins of any, they are retained" (John xx:23). The preaching of repentance and forgiveness of sin would be their mandate, even if they still did not entirely grasp it.

Forty days later, after having led them out of the city walls to just past Bethany—which meant He would have passed through the Garden of Gethsemane where, not so long ago, He had sweat blood and prayed that the chalice pass from Him—He had once before told some of them that they too would drink from the chalice. He was about to pass the chalice to them as He ascended.

The last thing He instructed was that they convert the world. The last thing He said was that He would be with them throughout all days until the end of time through the presence of the Spirit. The last thing He did was bless them. The commands of the King, the foretelling of the Prophet, the blessing of the Priest. The last moment His pierced feet graced the earth, He completed in Himself the office of Priest, Prophet, and King. On His followers He bestowed a share in His own dignity. They were to use it to preach repentance in His Name and forgiveness of sins, baptizing in the name of the Triune God. Their mission was souls, even if they still did not fully grasp it. In ten days' time, they would.

Since Our Blessed Lord is the same yesterday, today, and forever, His commands remain constant. He instructed the Apostles, and through them us, to teach the world everything He had commanded. He told them, and again, us, that they would be His witnesses to the ends of the earth. But the word "witness" has a far deeper meaning than just a person with some testimony. It means "martyr." What applied to the Apostles applies to us with regard to the mission.

Hate will surround the witness to Our Blessed Lord just as it surrounded Him. There is no such thing as a witness without a cross, just as there is no daytime without light. One reflects the other. We must realize this in our own lives. The Apostles had been prepared over forty days of instructions to receive the completeness of knowledge, no longer confined just to knowing about but knowing of Our Lord. They were instructed to take Him to the world, to the ends of the earth, and to the end of time. They needed one more lesson to graduate to witness, and that would happen in ten days' time.

Chapter 18

THE THIRD GLORIOUS MYSTERY:

The Descent of the Holy Spirit on Our Lady and the Apostles

Fifty days earlier, the Apostles had received a "breathing" of the Holy Spirit from Our Lord in the Upper Room. Now they were to receive power to execute the mission—a mission to extend Him to the four corners of time. His presence in bodily companionship was gone, true, but His presence would now continue in them. They would be His Body, as St. Paul would quickly come to learn and preach.

Following on St. Paul's teaching, we are each members of this Body, and the blood enduring in each cell is prayer. Prayer is what carries the spiritual nutrients to each member. Without blood, the body dies. No matter the current state of health, fitness, and robustness, the body deprived of blood quickly becomes a corpse and decomposes.

In an intuitive way, the Apostles knew this. It was further exhibited by the life of Our Blessed Mother around Whom they now gathered, failing the physical companionship of Her Divine Son—for She was both exemplar of prayer and the living, breathing person from Whom He had drawn His humanity, a humanity they had just witnessed ascending to Heaven and taking His seat on the throne.

What heady days these must have been for the small, infant Church, lying dormant in the womb of the Upper Room awaiting birth. The rush of information, the flood of grace, the physical presence of the Queen of Heaven—what else could they do but pray?

And the prayer they said, mystically, was the Rosary. For what is prayer other than the raising of the mind and heart to God? And how else are the mind and heart raised to God other than through the work of redemption, which brings the Spirit without Whom we cannot pray? So as the Apostles sat collected around their Holy Mother—for She had been given to all of them in the person of John, and by extension to all who would come to believe in their word—what they would have prayed about and contemplated was the life of Our Blessed Lord.

Our Lady would have spoken often of that first visit of Gabriel all those years ago and his magnificent announcement, of which they were all current participants. She would have spoken of John the Baptist and being the first to hold him as he came forth from Elizabeth. She would have told them there in the Upper Room of the encounter between Herself and Elizabeth and the power of the Holy Spirit on Whom they were waiting.

She would have relayed the story of Bethlehem, the Magi, the shepherds, the pronouncement of the angel over the nearby hills to those same shepherds. She would have described the prophecy of Simeon during the Presentation, when She and St. Joseph brought the Child to the Temple. And as they sat there, only a few streets away from the Temple, She would have recalled how She and Joseph scurried about the city for three days in search of their Son.

In Her immaculate presence, the first beads of the Joyful Mysteries were being strung together—so too the rest of the Rosary in its nascent form, beads still being strung together, links fastened. It mattered not that it would take more than a thousand years for it to come to the world in its present form. For everything, there is the time of preparation. The more perfect the prayer, the more power-ful the weapon, the more time at the forge is needed.

So here they sat, in contemplation, meditation, individually and collectively in prayer and reflection and rejoicing. They were obedi-ent servants doing what their Lord had commanded them: "stay in the city, until you are clothed with power from on high" (Luke xxiv:49). All future millennia of the Faith were being formed in that small Upper Room, collected into one everlasting blast of spiritual radiation that would topple empires, raise up saints from the dead bones of men, rock Hell to its foundations, and inaugurate the public face of the Kingdom of Heaven.

He had preached it, said it was already among them. But in Him it was hidden, veiled. Now it was visible and would forever remain so —the birth of the Church Militant armed to vanquish Hell, to extend the reign of its Master and General and King throughout all time and beyond. The eternal work of the Trinity was now accomplished in time. And so it would remain for every generation until there were no more generations.

The Catholic Church is this accomplished work—the work of beauty, the perfect artistry of the the Perfect Artisan. From all eternity, the Three Persons longed for Her, knew Her, incubated Her, and now She was brought forth, the Heavenly Jerusalem to supplant the soon-to-be destroyed earthly Jerusalem. What man had built could not contain God, as He had said to David, to Solomon. He would build His own house, His own Temple, and it would be His resting place forever, and the gates of no empire, not even the empire of Satan, would destroy it, for they would not be able to withstand Her. She would be on the offensive, throughout time, doing the work commanded of Her by Him as He raised His nail-scarred hands over Her. *Preach repentance and forgiveness of sins until the end of time and baptize. Save souls and lose your own selves in the process so you may become sons of the Father in the Kingdom prepared for you from the foundation of the world.*

This is the meditation of those who would pray the Glorious Mysteries. Yes, the Holy Spirit came down in time in Jerusalem, but He comes down in all time; there is never a time when He is not coming to us. We have to spend time learning and praying and witnessing—martyring. This is the glory of the Rosary: that we are given a weapon that can forge us, build us into a fortress of prayer, grace, a warehouse of graces, in fact, not just for our good, but for that of others.

Saint Peter kicked open the door on that birthday and confronted, challenged, did combat with, made war on conventional wisdom. He defended the joy of the Apostles, he derided the crowd for the scurrilous and slanderous charge that the band of his brother Apostles was drunk. He challenged them, cut them off, confronted them about the entire truth of Our Blessed Lord, accused them of His death, conquered them by preaching repentance and forgiveness of their sins by Him for them. "[A]nd there were added that day about three thousand souls" (Acts ii:41).

Such is the power of the Holy Spirit when longed for and when studied and prayed for. He bestows those seven gifts as the weaponry to change the world and attack the gates of Hell. And nothing can repel the overrunning of Hell, not even Hell itself. As a precursor to the final hour of the final day, St. John, who was present at Pentecost, foresaw the Heavenly Jerusalem coming down from the sky, adorned as a Bride to meet Her Groom. Years before he described that, he saw the beginning of it with his own blessed eyes in the Upper Room. How his thoughts must have never strayed far from the events of that feast of Pentecost.

This is our call, we baptized and confirmed, we Church Militant. A soldier prepares for battle by employing his weapon in readiness, cleanliness, maintenance, and practice. Soldiers of the Church Militant prepare for battle with the weapons of prayer, contemplation, reflection. Ours is to extend Christ until we see Him again.

Chapter 19

THE FOURTH GLORIOUS MYSTERY:

The Assumption of the Blessed Virgin Mary, Body and Soul, into Heaven

The point of reflection on combat in this mystery is victory. Our humanity, so despised by the enemy on every level, is raised to its final completeness in the Woman of Genesis. If every soul ever created were eventually damned, this solitary victory would cause him unending agony. He needs total victory over humanity. For him, even one soul who escapes him is final loss.

So when the Holy Trinity determined that the life of the Blessed Mother on earth was completed, They drew Her up, in Her complete humanity, to reign with Them forever. And not like the others —the saints, martyrs, prophets, patriarchs, Apostles—but uniquely.

To Her belongs the first taste of absolute and complete victory for the human race because the entirety of Her humanity is present to the Trinity in unending bliss. Her body is with Her—the tabernacle that brought Christ to the world, the lips that, by their instruction to the stewards at Cana, set Her Son's feet on the road to our redemption—all of Her is in Heaven.

The saints will one day as well have their bodies reunited to them, but this has already been accomplished in Mary as a forerunner of our everlasting destiny. We can look to Our Blessed Lord to see the victory accomplished; we can look to Our Blessed Mother to see the victory applied in human flesh. The Psalms point to Our Blessed Lord. He is buried in each one, sometimes clearly, other times obscurely, but He is present in each. Since those who attain to victory in Christ also share in the components of His life, then buried in Christ buried in the Psalms are we as well.

We will suffer for righteousness, be betrayed by those closest to us,

97

cry out to God feeling abandoned by Him. We will shout hymns of praise to Him, sing a new song, long for the courts of the Lord. The saved are in the Psalms because they are in Christ, configured to Our Blessed Lord. This is true of no one more than His own Mother. What applies to Him applies to Her, as it does for all of us.

She felt the full weight of the Cross particular to Her suffering, so we must as well. One psalm in particular helps us to focus our attention on this mystery of destiny, the destiny already achieved by the Queen of Heaven, where She continues to assist Her children in realizing their destiny. It is Psalm 16. It is the assurance that Christ will rise bodily from the grave, uncorrupted:

> Therefore my heart is glad, and my soul rejoices;
>   my body also dwells secure.
> For thou dost not give me up to Sheol,
>   or let thy godly one see the Pit. (Ps. xvi:9–10)

Saint Louis de Montfort said, "The 'Hail Mary' said well is the force that puts the devil to flight. It is the sanctification of the soul, the joy of the angels, the melody of the elect, the canticle of the New Testament, the delight of Mary, and the glory of the Holy Trinity." Why? Because Mary enjoys a unique relationship to the Holy Trinity that no other creature ever did or ever will. She is Daughter to the Father, Mother to the Son, and Spouse of the Spirit.

Because of this singular relationship, the Persons of the Trinity desired Her to be present to Them in Her completeness, which She now is. In this way, She is the exemplar for us, the model of what we will be. Her destiny is now Her reality, and Her reality is our destiny. At the end of the world, we too shall be assumed body and soul into Heaven.

At the Preface for the Mass on the Solemnity of the Assumption, the Church prays:

> For today the Virgin Mother of God
> was assumed into Heaven
> as the beginning and image

of your Church's coming to perfection
and a sign of sure hope and comfort to your pilgrim people;
rightly you would not allow Her
to see the corruption of the tomb
since from Her own body She marvelously brought forth
your incarnate Son, the Author of all life.

At some point in battle, soldiers and warriors must be given hope, have the plan of battle shown to them and the goal made clear. During World War II, American soldiers fighting on Iwo Jima were battle-weary and locked in a stalemate with the occupying Japanese forces. In a moment, they beheld the American flag unfurled atop Mt. Suribachi by a platoon of six marines from Easy Company, Second Battalion, 28th Marines.

Mount Suribachi was such a dominant height on the tiny island that it could be seen not just from the beaches, but also from the landing craft and the ships. The U.S. soldiers from every direction let out such loud cheers that the Japanese fighters, tucked away in a maze of tunnels and underground bunkers, were alerted and began a vicious counter-assault. (It took almost another month for the island to be secured, despite the fact that the flag was raised only a few days after the battle had begun.)

The island of Iwo Jima was the first land mass that was officially Japanese territory to be captured. Iwo was part of the prefecture of Tokyo and was the first homeland soil to be taken, so it was a matter of great honor for the Japanese forces to hold on to it and repel the invading Americans. The unfurling of the flag was a vision of victory for the American forces, even if the victory had not yet been realized for every Marine on the island.

For us, this is a parallel to the Assumption of Our Blessed Mother. Her Assumption is an unfurling of the banner of victory, a sign of our goal, our mission, for all of us still fighting here on earth. Victory is assured, guaranteed, promised, even if not yet fully realized. The Assumption is a looking forward, a glimpse into the future when all fighting will have ceased because there will no longer be an enemy to vanquish. As Mother Church so splendidly prays, "a sign of sure hope and comfort to your pilgrim people."

We are still engaged in intense combat, much of it hand-to-hand, and will be until we die. Yet the intensity is raised to a level of joy and inspiration when we can bring the "flying banner" to mind, held out to us by the Church, of Our Lady's victory, thus renewing our commitment to the fight. Just as the flag raised on Iwo Jima was the first victory on Japanese homeland soil, a stake driven into the ground, so too was it a sign of final and complete victory. As stated above, so precious was this strip of land to the Japanese that the fighting continued with greater ferocity for another month—even after the American flag had been raised.

When the demonic beholds the banner of final victory flying in Heaven, when the ancient enemy sees the One most hated by him in all creation, it is a constant reminder to him of his future. He knows he will be unable to destroy Her children forever, nor will he win all of them. Saint John, who wrote so profoundly of the Woman, draws the picture for us in his Apocalypse of the dragon waiting to devour the child as She gives birth. The child is snatched up to Heaven, and so he pursues Her into the desert, but She is protected and given refuge in a secret place prepared by God.

So John tells us the dragon goes in pursuit of Her children, and in one extremely telling line, he warns us, "But woe to you, O earth and sea, for the devil has come down to you in great wrath, because he knows that his time is short!" (Rev. xii:12). So the final victory is won. Satan can see it—enfleshed spirit assumed into Heaven—and it is impossible for him to deny his fate. The intensity will be ratcheted up. He cannot touch Her, but he will pursue Her offspring relentlessly, raging and frothing, breathing out fury, for his own nature, so thoroughly perverted, now knows no other way to behave than to destroy. All the while, amid his violence and fury, there flies the banner of victory atop the high point of his homeland, never able to be taken back, the first piece of his territory recaptured from him.

Chapter 20

THE FIFTH GLORIOUS MYSTERY:

The Crowning of the Blessed Virgin Mary as Queen of Heaven and Earth

In this final mystery, we combatants, we militants of the Holy Church, can meditate on the moment of laying down our weapons and coming into the presence of the Royal Court of the celestial. We shall meet our Queen, She Who sustained us in battle, prayed on our behalf to Her Son to give us renewed strength in our battles, Who dispensed to us every grace required. We who have spent time on earth as recipients of Her bounty will now behold the Great Giver of All Bounty, of All Grace face to face—Our Mother, the Queen!

How dearly did the Holy Trinity anticipate this moment in time, although the Persons had already beheld it in eternity. How much did they long to lay on the head of the most perfect, immaculate, beautiful creature Her crown, reserved for Her in Heaven from all eternity.

Never was it *not* the case that this thought was always present to the Father, Son, and Holy Spirit. But the thought became *experienced* in the glorified and assumed body of the Virgin. Whatever may have been lacking in Her vision of the Trinity while She walked the earth, however it may have been wanting, to whatever mode or type or degree, it was and is now fully completed and completely full. Mary is now completely "full of grace" inasmuch as She would have been when Gabriel came to Her all those decades earlier. Now Her Queenship is visible and proclaimed.

This is the moment of the future we can approach now in time. For while She will be Queen to us in a manner corresponding to our heavenly capacity to receive Her glory and majesty in eternity, we at this moment have the ability to participate fully in Her Queenship now, in our limited capacity. We may pray "Hail, Holy Queen" from such stirrings and depths that She, even now, increases our capacity to receive Her graces in preparation for our final destiny, so that we may be raised up to the highest level of glory of which we are capable. The graces She bestows on us now are ammunition to repel the invasion of the enemy. We belong to Her. We are Her offspring. We were given to Her by Her Son from the throne of His Cross when He gave care of John to Her.

Recall that the gospels tell us John's biological mother, Salome, was not only still alive but present at Golgotha. He needed no second mother, not in any earthly sense. But he did require a heavenly Mother, as do all engaged in battle with the enemy. She is our constant encouragement, our enforcer, our protector.

Part of a homily by St. Amadeus of Lausanne, a 12th-century bishop and crusader, no stranger to the royal courts of his day, is helpful here. He titled his homily "Queen of the World and of Peace":

> Observe how fitting it was that even before Her Assumption the name of Mary shone forth wondrously throughout the world. Her fame spread everywhere even before She was raised above the Heavens in Her magnificence. Because of the honor due Her Son, it was indeed fitting for the Virgin Mother to have first ruled upon earth and then be raised up to Heaven in glory. It was fitting that Her fame be spread in this world below, so that She might enter the heights of Heaven on overwhelming blessedness.

> Just as She was borne from virtue to virtue by the Spirit of the Lord, She was transported from earthly renown to heavenly brightness. So it was that She began to taste the fruits of Her future reign while still in the flesh. At one moment She withdrew to

God in ecstasy; at the next She would bend down to Her neighbors with indescribable love. In Heaven angels served Her, while here on earth She was venerated by the service of men. Gabriel and the angels waited upon Her in Heaven.

The virgin John, rejoicing that the Virgin Mother was entrusted to him at the Cross, cared for Her with the other Apostles here below. The angels rejoiced to see their Queen; the Apostles rejoiced to see their Lady, and both obeyed Her with loving devotion. Dwelling in the loftiest citadel of virtue, like a sea of divine grace or an unfathomable source of love that has everywhere overflowed its banks, She poured forth Her bountiful waters on trusting and thirsting souls.

Able to preserve both flesh and spirit from death, She bestowed healthgiving salve on bodies and souls. Has anyone ever come away from Her troubled or saddened or ignorant of the heavenly mysteries? Who has not returned to everyday life gladdened and joyful because his request had been granted by the Mother of God?

As Queen, Our Lady's primary duty in giving glory to God is to participate in His will, which is the salvation of souls. As Queen, Her authority and power are unmatched, and therefore She is Queen Most powerful. As Her children, we can look to Her not only for intercession, but also as a promise of final rest and victory.

She is, in one of Her many titles, Our Lady of Victory—but the victory is not isolated to a solitary victory here or there in time, but a foretaste of the complete and final victory in store for us who bow to Her as Queen, owing to the Kingship of Her Son.

EPILOGUE

The Great Chain

In the 1600s a young woman from Agreda, Spain took the habit and made her vows as a Franciscan nun. She eventually became the abbess of the Agreda Franciscan Monastery until she died in 1665. So renowned was she for her holiness that the process to have her canonized began almost immediately after her death. To this day, her mortal remains are incorrupt. During her life, she had experienced private revelations and mystical phenomena. The best-known of these events that she put down in writing is called *The Mystical City of God—Divine History of the Virgin, Mother of God.* Venerable Mary of Agreda relates that the book was dictated to her personally by Our Blessed Mother Herself.

As we conclude our examination of the sublime reality of the Holy Rosary, there are two parts of the book worth paying close attention to and reflecting on for all those who understand spiritual warfare and their duty to fight, especially as it relates to the Rosary.

What follows is an excerpt from Chapter 10 of *The Mystical City of God*:

> Lucifer and his demons in the course of the life and miracles of Our Savior never could ascertain fully whether the Lord was true God and Redeemer of the world, and consequently what the dignity of the most holy Mary was. This was so disposed by Divine Providence, in order that the whole mystery of the Incarnation and redemption of the human race might be more fittingly accomplished. Lucifer, although knowing that God was to assume human flesh, nevertheless knew nothing of the manner and the circumstances of the Incarnation. . . .

Lucifer and his demons, as soon as they saw the Lord taking the Cross upon His sacred shoulders, wished to fly and cast themselves into Hell: for at that moment they began to feel with greater force the operations of His divine power. By divine intervention this new torment made them aware that the death of this innocent Man, Whose destruction they had plotted and Who could not be a mere Man, threatened great ruin to themselves. They therefore desired to withdraw, and they ceased to incite the Jews and the executioners, as they had done hitherto.

But the command of the Most Blessed Virgin Mary, enforced by the divine power, detained them and, enchained like fiercest dragons, compelled them to accompany Christ to Calvary. **The ends of the mysterious chain that bound them was placed into the hands of Mary**, the great Queen, Who, by the power of Her Divine Son, held them all in subjection and bondage. Although they many times sought to break away and raged in helpless fury, they could not overcome the power of the Heavenly Lady. She forced them to come to Calvary and stand around the Cross, where She commanded them to remain motionless and witness the end of the great mysteries there enacted for the salvation of men and the ruin of themselves. (emphasis added)

The chain that held them bound and secured them in place to watch their ruin was the Rosary.

As a sweet chord of final victory in the great opus of spiritual war, reflect on the glory of God, transmitted in this section from the same chapter. It deals with the moment when Our Blessed Lord from the Cross said, "Woman, behold, your son!" (John xix:26).

At the third word spoken by the Lord to His Mother: "Woman,

behold your son!" the demons discovered that this Heavenly Lady was the true Mother of the God-Man, the same Woman Whose likeness and prophetic sign had been shown to them in the Heavens at their creation, and Who was to crush their heads as announced by the Lord in the terrestrial paradise. They were informed of the dignity and excellence of this great Lady over all creatures, and of Her power they were even now experiencing. As they had from the beginning of the world and from the creation of the first woman used their astuteness to find out Who this great Woman announced in the Heavens could be, and as they now discovered Her in Mary, Whom they had until now over-looked, these dragons were seized with inexpressible fury.

Pray the Holy Rosary every day, and remember its power.

APPENDIX

As I said at the beginning of the book, the Rosary had always been difficult for me owing to distractions. My brain is all over the place all the time, and trying to quiet it down and focus on something that is partially repetitious proved difficult—difficult, that is, until I began saying short passages from the Scriptures that relate to the individual mysteries in between each "Hail Mary."

While I sometimes vary which passages I use to help focus my meditations, here is a list that has helped me tremendously. I offer it to you in whatever way it might be helpful. Please offer a Rosary for me.

GOD love you.

Scripture Reflections for the Recitation of the Holy Rosary

THE JOYFUL MYSTERIES

1. The Annunciation

1. In the sixth month, the angel Gabriel was sent by God to a Virgin in the town of Nazareth Who was betrothed to a man named Joseph, who was of the house and lineage of David, and the Virgin's name was Mary.

2. And coming to Her he said, "Hail, full of grace, the Lord is with you."

3. "Do not be afraid, Mary, for You have found favor with God."

4. But She was greatly disturbed at his greeting and wondered what sort of greeting this might be.

5. "You shall conceive and bear a son, and You shall call His name Jesus, for He will save his people from their sins."

6. "But how can this be since I do not know man?"

7. "The Holy Spirit will come upon You and the power of the Most High will overshadow You; therefore, the Child born to You shall be called holy, the Son of the Most High God."

8. "And see, Elizabeth, Your kinswoman, has conceived a son in her old age. She who was thought barren is in her sixth month, for nothing shall be impossible for God."

9. "I am the handmaid of the Lord; be it done unto Me according to thy word."

10. And with that the angel left Her.

2. The Visitation

1. Mary set out in haste for the hill country.

2. And upon entering the house of Zechariah She called out to Elizabeth.

3. And when the sound of Her greeting reached Elizabeth's ears, the child in her womb leapt for joy.

4. And Elizabeth, filled with the Holy Spirit, said, "Blessed art thou among women and blessed is the fruit of thy womb."

5. "And blessed is she who believed that the Lord would fulfill his promise."

6. "And why is it that the Mother of my Lord should come to me?"

7. "For from the moment the sound of your greeting reached my ears the child in my womb leapt for joy."

8. And Mary cried out, "My soul magnifies the Lord and my spirit rejoices in God my savior."

9. "From henceforth all generations will call me blessed."

10. Mary stayed with Elizabeth about three months.

3. The Birth of Our Lord

1. In those days, Caesar Augustus sent out a decree that the whole world should be enrolled.

2. This was while Quirinius was governor of Syria.

3. So Joseph set out for Bethlehem with his wife who was with child, for he was of the house and lineage of David.

4. And while they were there, Her days of confinement came to an end and She brought forth Her firstborn Son and wrapped Him in swaddling clothes and laid Him in a manger because there was no room for them at the inn.

5. Now there were shepherds in the nearby hills keeping night watch over their flocks.

6. Suddenly the angel of the Lord appeared to them, and the glory of the Lord shone round them, and they were sore afraid.

7. "Fear not, for I bring you good news of glad tidings which shall be for all the people, for unto you this day is born in the city of David a Savior Who is Christ the Lord."

8. "And let this be a sign unto you: You shall find the Babe wrapped in swaddling clothes and lying in a manger."

9. Suddenly there was with the angel a whole multitude of the heavenly host singing glory to God in the highest and peace on earth to men of good will.

10. The shepherds went to Bethlehem and reported all that had happened, and Mary kept all these things and treasured them and reflected on them in Her heart.

4. The Presentation

1. When the forty days had passed, they took Jesus to the Temple to do for Him what was prescribed by the law.

2. Now there was an old man in the Temple named Simeon. He was a devout and upright man.

3. It had been revealed to him by the Holy Spirit that he should not taste death until he had set eyes on the Messiah.

4. Going over to them, he took the Babe in his arms and he looked up to Heaven and he blessed God.

5. "Lord, now you can dismiss your servant in peace. Your word has been fulfilled. For my own eyes have seen the salvation which You have prepared in the sight of every people."

6. "A light to reveal You to the nations and the glory of Your people Israel."

7. And handing the Babe back to them he blessed them.

8. And he said to Mary, "This Child shall be responsible for the rise and fall of many in Israel."

9. "A sign that is to be contradicted."

10. "And a sword Thine own heart shall pierce, and the secret thoughts of many will be laid bare."

5. The Finding of the Child Jesus in the Temple

1. When Jesus was twelve years old, as was their custom, they went up to Jerusalem for the feasts.

2. And when they were returning, supposing Him to be among family and friends, they searched for Him for a full day.

3. Returning to Jerusalem they searched for Him for three days and three nights.

4. At long last they came across Him in the Temple.

5. He was sitting among the doctors and teachers of the law.

6. He was asking them questions.

7. All who heard Him were amazed at Him.

8. "Son, why have you done this to us?"

9. "Did You not know I must be about My Father's business?"

10. And He went down to Nazareth with them, and He was obedient unto them. And He grew in grace and strength and wisdom in the sight of both God and man.

THE LUMINOUS MYSTERIES

1. The Baptism of Our Lord by John the Baptist

1. "Baptize me, John."

2. "It is You Who should be baptizing me."

3. "We must fulfill all righteousness."

4. So Jesus went down into the waters.

5. And when He emerged a voice was heard from Heaven.

6. "This is My beloved Son, in Whom I am well pleased."

7. And the Holy Spirit descended upon Him in the form of a dove.

8. And John said, "Behold, the Lamb of God."

9. And the Holy Spirit drove Him out into the desert.

10. And there He did battle with demons and wild beasts.

2. The Self-Manifestation of the Lord at the Wedding Feast at Cana

1. Now there was a wedding feast in Cana.

2. And the Mother of Jesus was there.

3. So too were Jesus and some of His disciples.

4. And the Mother of Jesus turned to Him and said, "They have no wine."

5. Jesus responded, "Woman, what to Thee to Me?"

6. "My hour has not yet come."

7. And She turned to the wine stewards and said, "Do whatever He tells you."

8. Jesus instructed them to fill the jars with water.

9. Then He told them to draw some out in a cup and give it to the captain of the feast.

10. Having tasted it, he said, "You have saved the best wine for last."

3. The Proclamation of the Kingdom and Call to Conversion

1. "Repent, for the Kingdom of Heaven is at hand."

2. "My Kingdom is not of this world."

3. And they mocked Him and said, "Hail, King of the Jews."

4. Jesus said, "Behold, the Kingdom of Heaven is among you."

5. "The Kingdom of Heaven is like a mustard seed."

6. "It is the smallest of all seeds, but when it grows it becomes the largest of all bushes, and the birds of the air come and make their nests in it."

7. "The Kingdom of God is like a merchant in search of fine pearls."

8. "Having found a pearl of great value he goes and sells all he has and buys that pearl."

9. "Again, the Kingdom of God is like a man who finds a treasure buried in a field."

10. "And having found the treasure he goes and sells all that he has so he can buy that field and own that treasure."

4. The Transfiguration

1. Jesus took Peter, James, and John up a high mountain.

2. And there He was transfigured before them.

3. His countenance changed and His clothes became dazzling white.

4. On either side of Him appeared Moses and Elijah.

5. They were speaking with Him about His upcoming exodus.

6. And Peter said, "Lord, it is good that we are here. Let us build three tents: one for you, one for Moses, and one for Elijah." But he did not know what he was saying.

7. While he was still speaking a cloud came and covered them.

8. They were filled with great fear, and a voice came from the cloud and said, "This is My beloved Son, in Whom I am well pleased. Listen to Him."

9. When they looked up, they saw no one but Jesus.

10. And He gave them strict instructions to tell no one of this until He had risen from the dead. And they asked each other what "risen from the dead" meant.

5. The Institution of the Holy Eucharist

1. "Amen, amen, I say to you: You did not come because you believed the signs, but because you had your fill of the loaves."

2. "What sign can you perform? Moses gave us manna in the desert."

3. He said to them, "Amen, amen, I say to you, it was not Moses who gave you bread in the desert to eat, but My Father Who is in Heaven."

4. "I Myself am the living bread come down from Heaven."

5. "Unless you eat the Flesh of the Son of Man and drink His Blood you shall not have life within you."

6. "He who eats My Flesh and drinks My Blood abides in Me and I in him."

7. "And I will raise him up on the last day."

8. "Eat My Flesh."

9. And He took the bread in His hands, blessed and broke it, and said, "This is My Body."

10. Then He took the cup and said, "This is the cup of My Blood, the Blood of the new and everlasting covenant."

THE SORROWFUL MYSTERIES

1. The Agony in the Garden

1. Jesus took Peter, James, and John further into the garden with him.

2. "My soul is sorrowful even unto to death."

3. "Stay here and pray that you may not be put to the test."

4. Then He withdrew about a stone's throw and fell to the ground, praying, "Father, if it be possible, let this cup pass Me by."

5. And His sweat became like great drops of blood falling to the ground.

6. Again He prayed, "Father, if it be possible, let this cup pass Me by."

7. Then He went back to the Apostles and found them sleeping. "Could you not stay awake with Me for one hour?"

8. A third time He went back and prayed, "Father, let this cup pass Me by; however, not My will, but Your will be done."

9. He returned to His Apostles and found them asleep. He said, "Still taking your rest. It is enough! Behold, My betrayer is at hand."

10. "Judas, you betray Your Master with a kiss?"

2. The Scourging at the Pillar

1. Now the whole cohort and the chief priests led Him to Pontius Pilate.

2. And Pilate came out to them and said, "What wrong has He done?"

3. "If He were not a criminal we would not have brought Him to you."

4. "We have a law, and according to this law He must die!"

5. So Pilate took Him inside and questioned Him. "Where do You come from?"

6. And Jesus made no answer. Pilate said, "Do You not know that I have the power to release You and the power to crucify You?"

7. "You would have no power over Me if it were not given to you from above. That is why he who handed Me over to you is guilty of the greater sin."

8. So Pilate went out and said to them, "I find no guilt in Him."

9. And Pilate looked for a way to release Him.

10. So he handed Him over to be scourged.

3. The Crowning with Thorns

1. The soldiers led Jesus into the praetorium.

2. And they wrapped Him in a purple cloak.

3. And they placed a reed into His hand.

4. And one of the soldiers fashioned a crown of thorns and pushed it onto His head.

5. And they knelt down before Him and mocked Him.

6. "All hail the King of the Jews!"

7. And they hit Him.

8. And they spat on Him.

9. And when they were done amusing themselves they put Him back into His own clothes.

10. And they led Him back to Pilate.

4. Carrying of the Cross

1. Pilate brought Him out and said, "Ecce homo! (Behold the Man!)"

2. And they yelled back, "Crucify Him!"

3. "Shall I crucify your king?"

4. "We have no king but Caesar!"

5. "This Man sets Himself up as a king. Anyone who sets himself up as king is a rival to Caesar."

6. So Pilate delivered Him up to their wishes.

7. And Jesus went out bearing His own Cross.

8. Along the way He met some women of Jerusalem who were crying and weeping. He said, "Do not weep for Me; weep rather for yourselves and for your children."

9. At last they arrived at the place of the skull, Golgotha in Hebrew. There they stripped Him of His garments.

10. And they crucified Him with two criminals, one on either side.

5. The Crucifixion and Death of Our Lord

1. And Pilate had a sign fixed to the Cross: "Jesus of Nazareth, King of the Jews."

2. And those who walked by mocked Him and said, "This Man said, 'Destroy this temple and in three days I will raise it up.'"

3. Others said, "Come down from the Cross and we will believe."

4. "Father, forgive them for they know not what they do."

5. "Today you shall be with Me in paradise."

6. "Woman, behold Your son. Son, behold your Mother."

7. "I thirst."

8. "My God, My God, why have You abandoned Me?"

9. "It is finished."

10. "Father, into Your hands I commend My spirit."

THE GLORIOUS MYSTERIES

1. The Resurrection

1. "Who will roll away the stone for us?"

2. "Why do you seek the living among the dead?"

3. "He is not here. He is risen."

4. "Mary!"

5. "How slow of heart and dull of mind you are."

6. "Did you not know the Christ must suffer, so as to enter into His glory?"

7. "And He took the bread, blessed it, broke it, and gave it to them."

8. Then He vanished from their sight.

9. And suddenly their eyes were opened and they recognized Him in the breaking of the bread.

10. Then He breathed on them and said, "Receive the Holy Spirit. Whose sins you forgive are forgiven them, whose sins you hold bound are held bound."

2. The Ascension

1. Jesus took them outside the city.

2. "All authority in Heaven and on earth has been given to Me."

3. "You shall be My witnesses throughout Judea, Samaria, and to the ends of the earth."

4. "Go, therefore, and teach all nations, baptizing them in the name of the Father, and of the Son, and of the Holy Spirit."

5. "Teach them to observe all that I have taught you."

6. "And know that I am with you all days, even unto the consummation of the world."

7. And while He was still speaking, a cloud came upon Him and took Him from their sight.

8. And they stood there looking up into the sky.

9. Suddenly two men in white appeared beside them.

10. "Men of Jerusalem, why do you stand here gazing up into the sky? This Jesus, Whom you saw leave will return to you in the same way."

3. The Descent of the Holy Spirit on Our Lady and the Apostles

1. As was their custom, they were gathered in the upper room praying.

2. Now there were Jews from every nation gathered in Jerusalem for the feast.

3. Suddenly, a sound like a loud rushing wind was heard throughout the house.

4. Those outside the house heard it as well.

5. And suddenly the Holy Spirit descended upon them in the form of tongues of fire, which came to rest over each one of them.

6. And they began to preach.

7. And the assembled Jews said, "How is it that we can each hear them speaking in our own native tongue?"

8. And Peter went out to the crowd and addressed them.

9. "This Jesus of Nazareth Whom you crucified God raised from the dead."

10. And that day about three thousand were added to their number.

4. The Assumption of the Blessed Virgin Mary, Body and Soul, into Heaven

1. Preserve my soul, O God, I take refuge in You.

2. I say to the Lord, You are my God. My happiness lies in You alone.

3. He has put into my heart a marvelous love for the faithful ones who dwell in His land.

4. Those who choose other gods increase their sorrows. Never will I offer their offerings of blood. Never will I take their name upon my lips!

5. Oh Lord, it is You Who are my portion and cup; it is You Yourself Who are my prize.

6. The lot marked out for me is my delight. Welcome indeed the heritage that falls to me!

7. I will bless the Lord Who gives me counsel, Who even at night directs my heart.

8. I will keep the Lord ever in my sight; since He is at my right hand, I shall stand firm.

9. And so my heart rejoices, my soul is glad; even my body shall rest in safety.

10. For You will not leave my soul among the dead, nor suffer Your beloved to know decay.

5. The Crowning of the Blessed Virgin Mary
as Queen of Heaven and Earth

1. Then a great sign appeared in the sky.

2. A Woman clothed with the sun.

3. With the moon under Her feet.

4. And over Her head a crown of twelve stars.

5. And God said to the serpent, "I will put hatred between you and the Woman."

6. "Between your offspring and Hers."

7. "You will strike at Her heel and She will crush your head."

8. And the angel said to Her, "The Lord God will give to Him the throne of His father David."

9. "And He will rule over the house of Jacob forever."

10. "And of His Kingdom there will be no end."